# Dou Catechism

## by Henry Tuberville, D.D.

# Table of Contents

# The Author to the Reader

The principle part of the Catechism is an Abridgment of the Christian Doctrine; defended and cleared by proofs of scripture, in points controverted between Catholics and Sectaries; and explained by the familiar way of question and answer.

To this, in the former impressions, was only adjoined a necessary exposition of the Mass, our Lady's Office, and the festival days of the year, but to this last edition is added, an Explanation of certain ceremonies of the Church, which now renders it more complete for instructing the ignorant, in the whole doctrine and discipline of the Catholic Church. Besides I have corrected some false citations, and other errata, which by the printer's negligence, occurred in the former impressions.

Peruse it, good reader, with such charity as I have penned it, and if by it perusal thou shalt become more knowing in the law of Christ, and in practice more dutiful to God, and thy neighbour, it will abundantly recompense the labour of Thy well-wishing friend

And servant in CHRIST

H T

# What a Christian is: And of the Blessed Trinity.

Q. 1. Quest. CHILD, What religion are you of?

Ans. Sir, by the benefit and grace of God, I am Christian.

Q. 2. Whom understand you by a Christian?

A. Him that inwardly believes and outwardly professes the law of Christ.

Q. 3. When are we obliged to make an external profession of it?

A. As often as God's honour, our own, or neighbour's good requires it.

Q. 4. How prove you that we are bound outwardly to profess our faith?

A. Out of St. Matt. x. 32, where Christ saith, Every one, therefore, that shall confess me before men, I will confess him before my Father who is in heaven. But he that shall deny me before men, I also will deny him before my Father who is in heaven.

Q. 5. Are we bound also to venture the ruin of our estates, the loss of our friends, and to lay down our very lives for the profession and defence of our faith?

A. Doubtless we are: seeing the reward we expect in heaven, infinitely exceeds all the pleasures and punishments of this life. And because Christ the Son of the living God, has suffered far greater things for us, even to a disgraceful death on the cross? and therefore, it were base ingratitude in us, not to be ready to give our lives for him as often as his honour shall require it. Luke, xiv. 26, 33.

Q. 6. In What doth the faith and law of Christ chiefly consist?

A. In two principle mysteries, namely, the unity and trinity of God, and the incarnation and death of our Saviour.

Q. 7. What means the unity and trinity of God?

A. It means, that in God there is but one only divine nature or essence, and that in the same one and divine nature there are three persons, the Father, and the Son, and the Holy Ghost.

Q. 8. How show you that?

A. Out of John, v. 7. There are three that give testimony in heaven, the Father, the Word, and the Holy Ghost, and these three are one.

Q. 9. Why are there but three Persons only?

A. Because the Father had no beginning, nor proceeds from any other person; the Son proceeds from the Father, and Holy Ghost proceeds from the Father and the Son.

Q. 10. What means the incarnation and death of our Saviour?

A. It means that the second person of the blessed Trinity was made man, and died on the cross to save us.

Q. 11. In What are these two mysteries signified?

A. In the sign of the cross, as it is made by Catholics, for when we put our right hand to our head, saying, In the name we signify Unity; and when we make the sign of the cross saying, Of the Father, and of the Son, and of the Holy Ghost, we signify Trinity.

Q. 12. How doth the sign of the cross represent the incarnation and death of our Saviour?

A. By putting us in mind that he was made man and died upon the cross for us.

## Faith Explained

Q. 13. What is faith?

A. It is a gift of God or a supernatural quality, infused by God into the soul, by which we firmly believe all those things which he hath any way revealed to us.

Q. 14. Is faith necessary to salvation?

A. It is; St. Paul assuring that without faith it is impossible to please God. Heb. xi. 6. and St. Mark, xvi. 16, saying, He that believeth not shall be condemned.

Q. 15. Why must we firmly believe matters of faith?

A. Because God hath revealed them, who can neither deceive, nor be deceived.

A second reason is, because not only all points of faith, but also the rule, or necessary and infallible means whereby to know them, to wit, the church's oral and universal tradition, are absolutely certain, and cannot lead us into error in faith; else we can never sufficiently be assured What is faith, or What is not.

Q. 16. If a man should deny, or obstinately doubt of some one point of faith, would he be thereby lose his whole faith?

A. Yes, he would; because true faith must always be entire, and he that fails in one, is made guilty of all, by discrediting the authority of God revealing it.

Q. 17. Is it not enough to believe all that is written in the Bible?

A. No, it is not: For we must also believe all apostolic tradition.

Q. 18. How prove you that?

A. Out of 2 Thess. ii. 15. Therefore brethren (saith St. Paul) stand and hold ye the traditions which ye have learned, whether by word, or by our Epistle.

Q. 19. What other proof have you?

A. The apostle's Creed, which all are bound to believe, although it be not in Scripture.

Q. 20. Is faith only, as excluding good works, sufficient to salvation?

A. No: it is not: St. James, ii. 24, saying, Do you see How that by works a man is justified, and not by faith only? And St. Paul, saying, 1 Cor. xiii. 2. If I should have all faith, so that I could remove mountains, and not have charity, I am nothing. And if I should distribute all my goods to feed the poor, and if I should deliver by body to be burned, and have not charity, it profiteth me nothing.

Q. 21. What faith will suffice to justify?

A. Faith working by charity in Jesus Christ.

Q. 22. What vice is opposite to faith?

A. Heresy.

Q. 23. What is Heresy?

A. Is it an obstinate error in things that are of faith.

Q. 24. Is it a grievous sin?

A. A very grievous one, because it wholly divides a man from God, and leads to atheism, Christ saying, if he will not hear the church let him be to thee as an heathen and a publican, Matt. xviii. 17.

# The Creed Expounded

Q. 25. What is the creed?

A. It is the sum of belief.

Q. 26. Who made it?

A. The twelve apostles.

Q. 27. At What time did they make it?

A. Before they divided themselves into the several countries of the world to preach the gospel.

Q. 28. For What end did they make it?

A. That so they might be able to teach one and the same doctrine in all places.

Q. 29. What doth the creed contain?

A. All those chief things which we are bound to believe, concerning God and his church.

## The First Article

Q. 30. What is the first article of the creed?

A. I believe in God the Father Almighty, Creator of heaven and earth.

Q. 31. What signifies I believe?

A. It signifies as much as I most firmly and undoubtedly hold.

Q. 32. What means, I believe in God?

A. It means that not only that I firmly believe there is a God, but also that I am piously affected to him, as to say chiefest good and last end, with confidence in him, or otherwise that I move unto him by faith, hope, and charity.

Q. 33. What signifies the word Father?

A. It signifies the first person of the most blessed Trinity, who by nature is the Father of his own only begotten Son, the second Person of the blessed Trinity; by adoption is the Father of all good Christians; and by creations is the Father of all creatures.

Q. 34. What means the word Almighty?

A. It means that God is able to do all things as he pleaseth; that he sees all things, knows all things, and governs all things.

Q. 35. Why is he called Almighty in this place?

A. That we might doubt of nothing which follows.

Q. 36. What signify the words, Creator of heaven and earth?

A. They signify that God made heaven and earth, and all creatures in them, of nothing, by his sole word, Gen. i.

Q. 37. What moved God to make them?

A. His own mere goodness, that so he might communicate himself to angels, and to men, for whom he made all other creatures.

Q. 38. When did God create the angels?

A. On the first day when he created heaven and earth, Gen. i. where Moses implies the creation of angels in the word heaven, and makes no other mention of it. The Nicene creed, interpreting the Apostles' Creed, says, that the words Creator of heaven and earth, mean all things visible and invisible.

Q. 39. For What end did God create them?

A. To be partakers of his glory, and our guardians.

Q. 40. How prove you by Scripture, that they be our guardians?

A. Out of St. Matt. xviii. 10, where Christ saith 'See that you despise not one of these little ones: For I day unto you, their angels in heaven always see the face of my Father who is in heaven.'

Q. 41. Do the angels know our necessities, and hear our prayers?

A. Doubtless they do, since God has deputed them to be our guardians; which is also proved out of Zach. i 12. where an angel prays for two whole cities; the words are 'Then the angel of the Lord answered and said, O Lord of hosts, How long wilt thou not have mercy on the cities of Juda and Jerusalem, against which thou hast been angry these seventy years?'

Q. 42. What Scripture have you for praying to angels?

A. Gen. xlviii. 16, where Jacob on his death bed prayed to an angel for Ephraim and Manasses, saying, 'The angel of the Lord that delivered me from all evils, bless these children.'

This place is cited for prayer to the angels in the notes of the Rhemish Testament upon it, and is confirmed to signify a created angel by St. Basil, lib. 3. cont. Dunon. sub initio: And St. Chrysosthom. 7. in laudem Sancti Pauli.

Q. 43. How did Lucifer and his fellow angels fall from their dignity in heaven?

A. By a rebellious sin of pride.

Q. 44. With What shall their ruins be repaired?

A. Will holy men.

Q. 45. When and to What likeness did God create man?

A. On the sixth day, and to his own likeness: Gen. i. 27.

Q. 46. In What doth the similitude consist?

A. In this, that man is in his soul an incorporeal, intellectual and immortal spirit, as God is. And in this, that as in God there is but one most divine nature or essence, and yet three distinct Persons; so in man there is but one indivisible soul, and yet in that soul three distinct powers, will, memory, and understanding.

Q. 47. How do you prove the soul to be immortal?

A. Out of Matt. x. 28, where Christ saith, 'Fear not them that kill the body, and cannot kill the soul.'

Q. 48. What other proof have you?

A. Out of Eccles. xii. 7. At our death the dust returns to the earth from whence it was, and the spirit to God that gave it.

Q. 49. In What state did God create man?

A. In the state of original justice, and perfection of all natural gifts.

Q. 50. Do we owe much to God for our creation?

A. Very much, seeing he made us in such perfect state, creating us for himself, and all things else for us.

Q. 51. How did we lose original justice?

A. By Adam's disobedience to God, in eating the forbidden fruit.

Q. 52. In What state are we now born?

A. In the state of original sin, and prone to actual sin, subject to death.

Q. 53. How prove you that?

A. Out of Rom. v. 12. 'By one man sin entered into the world, and by sin death; and so unto all men death did pass, in whom all have sinned.'

Q. 54. Had man ever died, if he had never sinned?

A. No, he had not, but had been converted by the tree of life, and been translated alive into the fellowship of the angels.

## The Second Article

Q. 55. Say the second article.

A. And in Jesus Christ his only Son our Lord.

Q. 56. Of What treats this article?

A. Of the second person of the blessed Trinity, in whom we also believe and put our trust.

Q. 57. What is the second Person?

A. He is true God, and true Man, in one Person.

Q. 58. How prove you that?

A. Out of St. John's Gospel, chap. i. 1. 'In the beginning was the Word, and the Word was with God, and the Word was God, &c. And the Word was made flesh, and dwelt among us.'

Q. 59. What other proof have you?

A. Out of Phil. ii. 6, 7, where St. Paul saith, 'That Christ when he was in the form of God, thought it not robbery to be equal with God, but he hath lessened himself, taking the form of a servant, made unto the likeness of men; and found in habit as a man.

Q. 60. Why should God be man man?

A. To redeem and save lost man.

Q. 61. Was his incarnation necessary for that end?

A. In the manner it was; because our offences against God were in some sort infinite; as being against his infinite goodness; and therefore required an infinite satisfaction; which no one could make but God and therefore he was made man.

Q. 62. What other proof have you for the necessity of the Incarnation?

A. Because God is in himself so spiritual, sublime, and abstract a thing, that if he had not in his mercy adapted his own inscrutable greatness to the littleness of our sensible capacity, by being made man, scarce on of a thousand would ever have been able to know anything to the purpose of him; or consequently to love and serve him as they ought, (which is the necessary means of our salvation) since nothing is efficaciously willed which is not first well understood.

Q. 63. What benefit have we by the knowledge of God made man?

A. It much inflames us with the love of God, who could not more have dignified men's nature, or shown more love to the world, then to send down his only Son to redeem it in our flesh.

Q. 64. What signifies the name of Jesus?

A. It signifies a Saviour, St. Matt. i. 21.

Q. 65. Is any special honour due to that name?

A. There is, because it is the highest title of God made man.

Q. 66. How prove you that?

A. Out of Phil. ii. 8, 9, 10, where we read, 'God hath given unto Christ because he hath humbled himself unto the death of the cross, a name which is above all names, the name of Jesus.'

Q. 67. What other proof have you?

A. Because there is no other name under heaven given to man, in which we must be saved. Acts iv. 12.

Q. 68. How prove you that we must bow at this name?

A. Out of Phil. ii. 10. That in the name of Jesus every knee should bow of those that are in heaven, on earth and in hell.

Q. 69. What signifies the name Christ?

A. It signifies anointed.

Q. 70. Why was he called anointed?

A. Because he was a priest, a prophet, and a king to all which unction pertains.

Q. 71. With What was Christ anointed?

A. With all the plenitude of divine grace.

Q. 72. What mean the words, his only Son our Lord?

A. They mean that Jesus Christ is the only Son of God the Father, begotten, as he is God, and of the same Father from all eternity, without a mother; and therefore is coequal and consubstantial to his Father; and consequently infinite, omnipotent Creator, and so Lord of us and all things, as the Father is.

## The Third Article

Q. 73. What is the third article?

A. Who was conceived by the Holy Ghost, born of the Virgin Mary.

Q. 74. What means, who was conceived by the Holy Ghost?

A. It means that the second Person of the blessed Trinity took flesh of the Virgin Mary, not by a human generation, but by the work of the Holy Ghost.

Q. 75. How prove you that?

A. Out of St. Luke i. 31, 35. Behold (saith the angel) thou shalt conceive and bear a Son, &c. the Holy Ghost shall come upon thee, and the virtue of the Highest shall overshadow thee.

Q. 76. What understand you by the words, born of the Virgin Mary?

A. I understand that Christ was born of her at midnight, in a poor stable at Bethlehem, between an ox and an ass.

Q. 77. Why at midnight?

A. To signify that he came to take away the darkness of our sins.

Q. 78. Why in Bethlehem?

A. Because it was the head city of David's family, and Christ was of David's race.

Q. 79. Why in a poor stable?

A. To teach us to love poverty and contempt of this world.

Q. 80. Why between an ox and an ass?

A. To fulfil that of the prophet, Thou shalt be known, O Lord, between two beasts, Habacuc xii. juxta Sept.

Q. 81. What doth the birth of Christ avail us?

A. It perfecteth in us faith, hope, and charity.

Q. 82. What signifies, "born of the Virgin Mary?"

A. It signifies that Our Lady was a virgin not only before, but also in, and after childbirth.

## The Fourth Article

Q. 83. What is the fourth article?

A. Suffered under Pontius Pilate, was crucified dead and buried.

Q. 84. What understand you by suffering under Pontius Pilate?

A. I understand that Christ, after a painful life of thirty-three years, suffered most bitter torments under the wicked president Pontius Pilate.

Q. 85. Where did he begin those sufferings?

A. In the garden of Gethsemani; that as sin began in the garden by the first Adam, so might grace also, by the second.

Q. 86. What are those torments?

A. His bloody sweat, his whipping at the pillar, his purple garment, his crown of thorns, his Sceptre of a reed, his carrying the cross, and many others.

Q. 87. What understand you by the words, was crucified?

A. I understand, he was nailed to a disgraceful cross between two thieves, for our offences, and to save us.

Q. 88. Is is lawful to honour the cross?

A. Yes, with a relative honour it is, because it is a special memorial of our Saviour's passion, and is called the sign of the Son of man, St. Matt. xxiv. 30.

Q. 89. What other reason have you?

A. Because the cross was the sacred altar, on which Christ offered his bloody sacrifice.

Q. 90. What scripture have you for it?

A. Gal. vi. 14. 'God forbid, (saith St. Paul,) that I should glory, but in the cross of our Lord Jesus Christ.'

Q. 91. What other proof have you?

A. Out of Phil. iii. 18. Many walk (saith St. Paul) of whom I have often told you, and now again weeping, I tell you that they are enemies to the cross of Christ, &c. whose end is perdition. And out of Ezek. ix. 4, where we read, That such as were signed with the sign Tau, (which was a picture and figure of the cross,) were saved from the exterminating angel, and only such.

Q. 92. What signifies the word dead?

A. It signifies that Christ suffered a true and real death.

Q. 93. Why was it requisite he should die?

A. To free us from the death of sin.

Q. 94. Why died he, crying with a loud voice?

A. To show he had power of his own life; and he freely gave it up for us, being strong and vigorous.

Q. 95. Why died he bowing down his head?

A. To signify his obedience to his Father, in the acceptance of his disgraceful death.

Q. 96. What means buried?

A. It means, that his body was laid in a new sepulchre, and buried with honour, as the prophet had foretold, Isa. xi. 10.

## The Fifth Article

Q. 97. What is the fifth article?

A. He descended into hell, the third day he arose again from the dead.

Q. 98. What means, he descended into Hell?

A. It means, that as soon as Christ was dead, he descended into Limbo, to free the holy fathers who were there.

Q. 99. How prove you that?

A. Out of Acts ii. 24, 27. 'Christ being slain, God raised him up loosing the sorrows of hell, as it was foretold by the prophet,' Psalm xv. 10. 'Thou wilt not leave my soul in hell, nor wilt thou give thy Holy One to see corruption.'

Q. 100. What other proof have you?

A. Ephes. iv. 8, 9. 'He ascending on high, hath led captivity captive; he gave gifts to men; and that he ascended,' What is it but because he descended into the lower parts of the earth?

Q. 101. Did he not descend to purgatory to free such as were there?

A. It is most probable he did according to 1 Pet. iii. 19, 20. 'Christ being dead, came in spirit; and preached to them also that were in prison, who had been incredulous in the days of Noah, when the ark was building.'

Q. 102. What understand you by, on the third day he rose again from the dead?

A. I understand, when Christ had been dead part of three days, on the third day, which was Sunday, he raised up his blessed body from the dead.

Q. 103. Why did he not raise it again sooner?

A. To testify that he was truly dead, and to fulfil the prophecies.

Q. 104. Did he reassume all the parts of his body?

A. He did, even to the last drop of his vital blood, and the very scattered hairs of his head.

Q. 105. Why did he retain the stigmas and marks of the sacred wounds?

A. To confound the incredulity of men, and to present them often to his Father, as a propitiation of our sins.

Q. 106. What benefit have we by the resurrection?

A. It confirms our faith and hope, that we shall rise again from death: 'For he who raised up Jesus will raise us also with Jesus.' 2 Cor. iv. 14.

## The Sixth Article

Q. 107. What is the sixth article?

A. He ascended into heaven, sits on the right hand of God the Father Almighty.

Q. 108. What means, He ascended into heaven?

A. It means that when Christ had conversed forty days on earth with his disciples, after his resurrection, teaching them heavenly things, then he ascended triumphant into heaven, by his own power.

Q. 109. From What place did he ascend?

A. From the top of the Mount of Olivet, where the print of his blessed feet are seen to this day.

Q. 110. Why from thence?

A. That were he began to be humbled by his passion, there he might also begin to be exalted.

Q. 111. Before whom did he ascend?

A. Before his mother, apostles and disciples, Acts 1. 9, &c.

Q. 112. In What manner did he ascend?

A. Lifting up his hands, and blessing them.

Q. 113. Why is it added, Into Heaven?

A. To draw our hearts to heaven after Him; 'If ye have risen with Christ, seek ye the things which are above.' Col. iii. 1.

Q. 114. What understand you by, Sits at the right hand of God?

A. I do not understand, that God the Father hath any hands, for he is incorporated, and a spirit: but that Christ is equal to his Father in power and majesty, as he is God; and that as man he is the highest created glory.

## The Seventh Article

Q. 115. What is the seventh article?

A. From thence he will come to judge the living and the dead.

Q. 116. What understand you by this article?

A. I understand Christ will come at the last day from heaven, to judge all men according to their work.

Q. 117. Does every man receive a particular judgment at his death?

A. He doth, but in the general judgment we shall be judged not only in our souls, as at our death, but also in our bodies.

Q. 118. Why is that necessary?

A. That as Christ was openly rejected, so he may there be openly acknowledged to the great joy and glory of his friends, as also to the confusion of his enemies.

Q. 119. How prove you that in the judgment all men shall receive according to their works?

A. Out of 2 Cor. v. 10. 'We must all be manifested (saith St. Paul) before the judgment seat of Christ, that every one may receive the proper things of the body according as he hath done, whether good or evil.' And out of St. Matt. xvi. 27. 'The Son of man (saith out Lord) shall come in the glory of his Father, with his angels, and then he will render to every one according to his works.'

Q. 120. Is there any merit in our good works?

A. There is, according to Apoc. xxii. 12. Behold I come quickly (saith the Lord) and my reward is with me; to render to every man according to his works.'

Q. 121. In What place shall this judgment be made?

A. In the Valley of Jehosaphat, as many suppose between Jerusalem and Mount of Olivet.

Q. 122. How prove you this?

A. By its conformity to that of the prophet. I will gather together all nations, I will send them into the Valley of Jehosaphat, and there will I plead with them upon my people, and my inheritance Israel,' Joel iii.

Q. 123. What signs shall go before it?

A. The sun and moon shall lose their lights, there shall be wars, plagues, famines, and earthquakes, in many places.

Q. 124. In What manner will Christ come unto it?

A. In great power and majesty, attended with legions of angels.

Q. 125. Who are they that shall be judged?

A. The whole race and progeny of man.

Q. 126. What are the things that shall be judged?

A. Our thoughts, words, and works, even to the secrets of our souls.

Q. 127. Who will accuse us?

A. The Devils, and our own guilty consciences: in which all our thoughts, words and deeds shall presently appear, and be laid open to the whole world.

Q. 128. How shall the just and reprobate be placed?

A. The just shall be on the right; the reprobate on the left hand of the Judge.

Q. 129. What shall be the sentence of the just?

A. 'Come, O ye blessed of my Father, and receive ye the kingdom which is prepared for you, for I was hungry and ye gave me to eat, I was thirsty, and ye gave me to drink,' &c St. Matt. xxv. 35, 36.

Q. 130. What shall be the sentence of the reprobate?

A. 'Go ye cursed into eternal fire, which hath been prepared for the devil and his angels; for I was hungry, and ye gave me not to eat,' &c. the same chap. v. 41, 42. You see of What weight good works will be at that day.

Q. 131. Why is it added, the living and the dead?

A. To signify that Christ shall judge, not only such as are living at the time of his coming, but likewise all such as have been dead, from the creation of the world; as also by the living, are understood angels and saints, by the dead, devils and damned souls.

## The Eighth Article

Q. 132. What is the eight article?

A. I believe in the Holy Ghost.

Q. 133. Of What treats this article?

A. Of the third Person of the blessed Trinity, in whom we also believe and put our trust, who proceeds from the Father and the Son, and is the self-same God with them, distinct in nothing but in person.

Q. 134. How prove you that?

A. Out of 1 John v. 7. 'There are three that give testimony in heaven, the Father, the Word, and the Holy Ghost, and these three are one.'

Q. 135. Why is the name of the Holy Ghost appropriated to the third Person, since angels are all spirits and holy?

A. Because he is such by excellency and essence, they only by participation.

Q. 136. At least Why should it not be common to the other two persons?

A. Because they are known by the proper names of Father and Son, but we have not any proper name for the Holy Ghost.

Q. 137. In What forms has the Holy Ghost appeared unto man?

A. In the form of a dove, to signify the purity and innocence which he caused in our souls; and in the form of a bright cloud, and fiery tongue, to signify the fire of charity, which he produced in our hearts, as also the gift of tongues; and hence it is, he is painted in these forms.

## The Ninth Article

Q. 138. What is the ninth article?

A. I believe in the holy Catholic Church, the communion of saints.

Q. 139. What understand you by this?

A. I understand that Christ hath a church upon earth which he established in his own blood, and that he hath commanded us to believe that church, in all things appertaining to faith, and morals, Matt. xviii. 17.

Q. 140. What kind of faith must we believe her with?

A. With the same faith that we believe her Spouse the Son of God, that is, with divine faith, but with this difference among other, that we believe in God; but though we believe the church, yet we do not properly believe in the church.

Q. 141. What is the church?

A. It is the congregation of all the faithful under Jesus Christ, their invisible head, and his vicar upon earth, the Pope.

Q. 142. What are the essential parts of the church?

A. A Pope or supreme head, bishops, pastors, and laity.

Q. 143. How prove you that bishops are of divine institution?

A. Out of Acts xx. 28. Take heed unto yourselves, and to the whole flock, wherein the Holy Ghost hath placed you bishops, to rule the church of God, which he hath purchased with his own blood.

Q. 144. How believe you St. Peter, and the Pope his successor, to be the visible head of the church?

A. First out of St. John xxi. 16, 17, and 18, where Christ gave St. Peter (for a reward of his special faith and love) absolute power to feed and govern his whole flock, saying, Feed my Lambs, feed my lambs, feed my sheep; therefore the rest of the apostles were his sheep, and he their head or pastor.

Secondly, out of St. Matt. xvi. 18, where Christ saith, Thou art Peter, and upon this Rock will I build my church. Therefore the rest of the apostles were built on him; and hence also it is, that in Scripture, St. Peter is still named first.

Q. 145. What are the marks of the true church?

A. Unity, sanctity, universality, and to be apostolical.

Q. 146. What mean you by the church's unity?

A. That all her members live under one evangelical law, obey the same supreme head, and his magistrates profess the same faith, even to the last article, and use the same sacraments and sacrifices.

Q. 147. How prove you out of Scripture that the church is one?

A. 1 Cor. x. 17. Being many (saith St. Paul) we are one bread, one body, all who participate of one bread.

Q. 148. Why may not a well-meaning person be saved in any religion?

A. Because there is but one Lord, one faith, one baptism, Ephes. iv. 5, and without (that one) faith, it is impossible to please God. Heb. xi. 6.

Q. 149. What other reason have you for it?

A. Because, as in a natural body, that part which has not a due connection to the heart or root, presently dies for want of continuity; so in the church (the mystical body of Christ) that man who has not a due subordination and connection to the head and common councils thereof, (that is, the Pope and general councils from whence under Christ we have our spiritual life and motion, as we are Christians,) must needs be dead, nor indeed can he be accounted a member of that mystical body.

Q. 150. Who, I beseech you, are those who are not to be accounted members of the Church?

A. All such as are not in the unity of the church, by a most firm belief of her doctrine, and due obedience to her pastors; as Jews, Turks, Heretics, &c.

Q. 151. Why may not Heretics and Schismatics justly claim to be in the Unity of the Church and Members of Christ's body?

A. Because Catholics can show to each sect of Heretics and Schismatics the time they began; the date of their separation from the Church: the name of the person or persons of their sect who first separated themselves, and the cause of their condemnation; whilst the Catholic Church always was from the beginning.

Q. 152. What if a Protestant should tell you, that the difference between them and us, are not differences in fundamentals, or in faith, but in opinion only, and therefore do not exclude them out of unity of the Catholic Church?

A. I should answer, they contradict themselves; for they accuse us of robbing God of his honour, in holding priestly absolutions from sins; in adoring Christ's body and blood, as really present in the eucharist, and holding the Pope's supremacy in things belonging to the spiritual government of the Church, also the infallibility of the Church and general councils, in delivering and defining points of faith, which are no matters of indifference, but high fundamentals.

Q. 153. How do you prove all obstinate Innovators to be Heretics?

A. Because they wilfully stand out against the definitive sentence of the Church of God, and submit not to any tribunal appointed by Christ to decide religious controversies; but follow their own interpretation of the dead letter of the scriptures.

Q. 154. And is not this the reason also Why Protestants and all other sectarians are so divided in religious matters?

A. Yes, it is; for How is it possible that people who imagine that there is no person or tribunal, or even the Church of God, infallible, for expounding the bible; people, who expound it each according to his respective fancy; people, who have no control over the erroneous interpretation of each other; How it is possible that such people would have the unity of faith, in the bond of peace; or that they be not tossed to and fro, and carried about with every wind of doctrine?

Q. 155. Why may not the letter of the Scripture be a decisive judge of controversies?

A. Because it has never been able from it[s] first publication, to decide any one dispute; as the whole world knows from experience: all heretics equally pretend to scripture authority in defence of their errors and heresies.

Q. 156. How then can we ascertain the truth amidst conflicting opinions?

A. By the infallible authority, definition, and proposition of the Catholic Church.

Q. 157. For What end, then, was the Scripture written, if not to be a decider of controversies?

A. The writing of the Holy Scriptures was for the purpose of the better preserving the revealed will of God, and that by a sensible and common reading of it, without any critical or controversial disputes of words, we might be able to know that God is, and What he is, and also that there is a heaven and a hell, rewards for virtue and punishment for vice, with examples of both, all which we find in the letter of the Scripture, by a plain and ordinary reading.

Q. 158. Is the church we speak of visible?

A. She is and must be visible at all times, as consisting of a hierarchy of pastors, governing, teaching, administering sacraments to the world's end, and of other people governed, taught and receiving sacraments at their hands, all publicly professing the same faith, all which things are visible.

Q. 159. How prove you that?

A. First, out of Eph. iv. 1, and 12. 'Christ gave some apostles, some evangelists, some doctors, some pastors, to the consummation of the saints, to the edifying of the body of Christ, and to the work of the ministry, until we all meet in the unity of faith.' Secondly, out of St. Matt. v. 14, where Christ saith of his church, "You are the light of the world, a city seated on a high mountain cannot be hid."

Q. 160. Why then would the Protestants have the church to be invisible?

A. Because we have convinced them, that there were no Protestants to be seen or heard of in the world before Martin Luther.

Q. 161. Why is the church said to be holy, or to have sanctity?

A. Because she hath a holy faith, a holy law, holy sacraments, and is guided by the Holy Ghost, to all truth and holiness.

Q. 162. How else prove you her sanctity?

A. Because Christ gave himself for his church that he might sanctify her, cleansing her by the laver of water in the world, that he might present her to himself a glorious church, not having spot or wrinkle, but that she might be holy and unspotted. Eph. v. 26, 27.

Q. 163. Notwithstanding the sanctity of the Catholic Church, are not some Catholics as wicked as Protestants?

A. Yes, verily, and more wicked, for where sanctity is less, their sacrilege cannot be so great. No man could damn his own posterity, but he that had original justice to lose: nor any man to betray Christ, but he that had eaten at his table. Protestants have not a holy faith, such sacraments, nor a holy church to abuse, as Catholics have, and therefore no wonder, if some Catholics be worse than any Protestants; yet Catholics have some saints, but Protestants have none.

Q. 164. Is the church infallible?

A. She is, and therefore to be believed, and all men may rest securely on her judgment.

Q. 165. How prove you that?

A. First, because she is the pillar and ground of truth 1 Tim. iii. 15.

Secondly, out of St. Matt. xvi. 18, where Christ saith, "Upon this Rock will I build my church, and the gates of hell shall not prevail against her."

Thirdly, out of St. John, xiv. 26. But the Paraclete, (saith he,) the Holy Ghost, shall teach you all things Whatsoever I shall say to you. And xvi. 13. But when the Spirit of truth cometh, he shall teach you all truth.

Q. 166. How declare you that the definitions of a council perfectly ecumenical, that is, a general council approved by the Pope, are infallible in matters of faith?

A. Because such a council is the church representative, and has the same infallibility that the church spread over the world hath.

Q. 167. What other reason have you?

A. Because of the definitions of such a council are the dictates of the Holy Ghost, according to that of the apostles, deciding in council, it hath seemed good to the Holy Ghost, and to us, Acts xv. 28.

Q. 168. What think you then of such as accuse the church of errors in faith and idolatry?

A. Truly I think them to be Heretics or Infidels, for our Lord saith, He that will not hear the church let him be unto thee as a heathen and a publican, St. Matt. xviii. 17.

Q. 169. Is not the church at least too severe in its censures and excommunications against sectaries?

A. No, she is very reasonable and charitable in them for vicious, passionate, and selfinterested men some times are brought to reason for fear of punishment and are forced to their own good, when no authority ordained by Christ is able to persuade them to it.

Q. 170. What understood you by the word catholic, or by the universality of the church?

A. I understand the church is universal, both for time and place.

Q. 171. How for time?

A. Because she hath been from Christ to this time, and shall be from thence to the end of the world.

Q. 172. How prove you that?

A. Out of St. Matt. xxviii. 20. Going therefore (saith our Lord) teach ye all nations, &c. and behold I am with you all days, even to the consummation of the world.

Q. 173. What mean you by the universality of place?

A. First, out of St. Matt. above cited, Teach all nations.

Secondly out of Psalm lxxxv. 9. All Nations, Whatsoever thou hast made, shall come and adore before thee, O Lord.

Thirdly, out of Apoc. vii. 9, where we read, that the church shall be gathered out of all nations, people, tribes, and tongues.

Q. 174. Why do we call the church the Roman Church?

A. Because, since the transition of St. Peter's chair from Antioch to Rome, the particular Roman Church has been head of all the churches, and to her the primacy has been affixed.

Q. 175. What is the rule by which the church preserves entire the deposit of Faith and confounds all sectaries?

A. Apostolical traditions, or receipt of doctrine by hand to hand from Christ and his apostles.

Q. 176. How prove you that?

A. Out of Rom. vi. 17. "Therefore I beseech you, brethren (saith St. Paul) mark them which make dissensions and scandals, contrary to the doctrine which you have learned, and avoid them, for such do not serve Christ our Lord."

Q. 177. What other proofs have you?

A. Out of St. Paul, saying, "But although we or an angel from heaven evangelize to you, besides that which we have evangelized to you, be he anathema, or besides, What you have received be he anathema." Gal. i. 8, 9.

Q. 178. Can the church err in faith, standing to this rule, and admitting nothing for faith, but What is consented by the whole church to have been so received?

A. She cannot, otherwise the whole church must there conspire in a notorious lie, to damn herself and her posterity, or else she must be ignorant What hath been taught for her faith by the church of the precedent age, which are both natural impossibilities.

Q. 179. How prove you these to be impossibilities by nature?

A. By the constancy and immutability of contingent causes, whose particulars may be defective, but the universals cannot.

Q. 180. Explain that a little.

A. Because one man or two or three may be born but with one arm, or one eye only, through defect of their particular causes; but that all nature should fail at once, and all men be so born, is totally impossible in nature; in like manner, one man or two may conspire in palpable lies to damn themselves and their posterity, or be deceived in What hath been taught them for faith, from their very cradles; but that the whole church should so far break with the nature of man (which is reason) to conspire in such a lie, or to be so mistaken, is as impossible in nature, as it is for men to be no men.

Q. 181. May some errors have been received for faith, and crept insensibly over the whole church, no man perceiving or taking notice of them?

A. No, that is as impossible as that the plague or burning fever should infect or spread itself over a whole kingdom for many years, no man perceiving it, or seeking to prevent it; for nothing causes greater notice to be taken, than any public or notorious change in matters of religion.

Q. 182. May not the power of temporal princes, or the over prevalency of human wit and reason, have introduced errors into the church?

A. Neither is that possible, seeing we are not regulated in things which are of faith, either by power, or any strength of reason, but by the rule of apostolical tradition, and by inquiring of the whole church of every age, What hath been taught by our forefathers, from Christ and his apostles.

Q. 183. Was not the Millenary heresy an apostolical tradition?

A. No, it was not; for there is no assurance or consent among those who write of it, that it was ever preached or delivered by the apostles. Q. 184. Did not St. Austin and Innocentius, with their councils, hold the communion of children a thing necessary to their salvation?

A. They speak not of sacramental communion, as is evident to all who have read their works, but of the effect of it, that is, of their incorporation into the mystical body of Christ, which is made in baptism, and this only they affirmed to be necessary to their salvation.

Q. 185. At least do not heretics say and aver, that the church hath apostatized and erred in faith?

A. They do indeed, but it will not serve their turn barely to say it, unless they were also able to prove it, (which they neither are or will be) by evident and undeniable proofs.

Q. 186. How prove you that?

A. First, because that presumption and possession of her integrity and infallibility is on the church's side; and therefore ought not to be yielded up, without clear evidence of her prevarication.

Secondly, because he that accuses his neighbour's wife of adultery, without convincing proof thereof, is not to be hearkened unto, but to be hated by all good men, as a most infamous slanderer; much more ought they who shall accuse the church, the spouse of Christ, of errors and apostasy, unless their proofs be evident and undeniable, to be detested as blasphemous heretics.

Thirdly, because if less than manifest and convincing evidence be sufficient to prove matters of this high nature, it is not impossible but every false tongue shall set dissensions between man and wife, and stir up the most faithful subjects in the world to a rebellion against their princes, both spiritual and temporal.

Q. 187. What other reason have you yet, Why the church and law of Christ may not fail and be utterly extinguished?

A. Because the causes of religion (to wit, the hope of good, and fear of evil from God) are universal and necessary, always knocking at men's hearts, and putting them in mind of some good or other, and therefore must needs have perpetual and necessary effects, which in such as are convinced that Christ is God, can be no other than the faith, hope and love of Christ, and the observance of his law, and that for ever, speaking of the whole church, although particular men may err and fall away.

Q. 188. What is it for the church to be apostolical?

A. To have been begun and propagated by the apostles, and to have a succession of pastors, and doctrines from them.

Q. 189. What means the communion of saints?

A. It means first that the faithful do all communicate in the same faith and sacraments, in the same sacrifice, and also in the merits of one another.

Q. 190. How prove you that?

A. Out of 1 Cor. xii. 26. And if one member suffer any thing, all the members suffer with it; or if one member do glory, all the members rejoice with it, you are the body of Christ, and members of a member.

Secondly, It means that the faithful on earth communicate with the angels and the saints in heaven; we by praising and praying to them, they by praying for us.

Q. 191. How do you prove this communion?

A. Out of Luke xv. 10. There is joy before the angels of God upon one sinner that doth penance. And out of 1 John i. 3, That you also may have fellowship with us, and our fellowship may be with the Father and with his Son Jesus Christ.

Q. 192. How prove you that the saints have any power to do us good?

A. Out of Apoc. ii. 26, 27, where Christ hath promised them power over us: to him, said he, that shall overcome, and keep my works to the end, to him will I give power over nations, and he shall rule them with an iron rod.

Q. 193. How prove you that it is lawful to pray to angels?

A. Out of Apoc. i. 4, where St. John did it: Grace (saith he) to you, and peace from him that is, that was, and that shall come, and from the seven spirits that are in the sight of his throne.

Q. 194. What other proof have you?

A. Out of Apoc. viii. 4, where we read, that they present the church's prayers to God. The smoke of the incense of the prayers of the saints ascend from the hand of the angel before God.

Q. 195. How prove you that we may pray to saints?

A. Out of Gen. xlvii, 16, where Jacob taught his children to do it, saying, And let my name be invocated upon them, the names also of my fathers, Abraham and Isaac. How prove you that they pray for us?

A. Out of Apoc. v. 8. The twenty-four elders fell down before the Lamb, having every one harps, and vials full of odours, which are the prayers of the saints.

Q. 196. Is it no dishonour to God, for us to pray to saints to pray for us?

A. No, it is not, nor yet to beg it of men; for St. Paul did it: We hope (saith he) that God will deliver us, you also helping in prayer for us. 2 Cor. i. 11.

## The Tenth Article

Q. 197. What is the tenth article?

A. The forgiveness of sins.

Q. 198. What do you understand by this?

A. I understand that God is both able and willing to forgive our sins, if we be heartily sorry for them, and confess them; and have given power to his church to remit them by baptism and penance.

Q. 199. How prove you that?

A. Out of Matt. ix. 8, where it is recorded by the Holy Ghost, that the multitude glorified God, who hath given such power unto man, as to forgive sins, (Christ having before proved the said power by a miracle) ver. 6, 7.

Q. 200. Is any sin so great that God cannot forgive it?

A. No there is not; for his mercy is far above our malice.

Q. 201. Can any one mortal sin be remitted without the rest?

A. It cannot, because the remission of mortal sin is a renewing of friendship with God by his grace, which can never be effected, so long as there remains in us any mortal sin.

Q. 202. Can we have absolute certainty, that our sins are forgiven us?

A. Without special revelation we cannot: I am not guilty in conscience (saith St. Paul) of any thing, but herein I am not justified. 1 Cor. iv. 4.

Q. 203. What other proof have you?

A. Because a man knows not whether he be worthy of love or hatred. Eccl. i. 9.

Q. 204. Can we be certain of our final perseverance?

A. Not without special revelation, and therefore St. Paul said, I chastise my body and bring it into subjection, lest when I preach to others I myself become a reprobate, 1 Cor. ix. 27, and Phil. ii. 12. He exhorts, saying, with fear and trembling, work out your salvation.

Q. 205. How then shall we have peace of conscience?

A. Because we may have moral certainty and a most lively hope, that our sins are forgiven by us by the due use of the sacraments, which is enough for our peace.

## The Eleventh Article

Q. 206. What is the eleventh article?

A. The resurrection of the flesh.

Q. 207. What means this article?

A. It means that these very bodies in which we now live, shall at the day of judgment be all raised up from death to life.

Q. 208. By What means shall this be done?

A. By the omnipotent command of God, and the ministry of angels.

Q. 209. How prove you that?

A. Out of 1 Thess. iv. 16. For our Lord in commandment, and in the voice of an archangel, and in the trumpet of God, will descend from heaven, and the dead that are in Christ shall rise again.

Q. 210. Shall the same bodies rise again?

A. The same in substance, though different in qualities.

Q. 211. How prove you that?

A. Out of Job xix. 25, 26, 27. For I know that my Redeemer liveth, and in the last day I shall rise out of the earth, and shall be compassed again with my skin, and in my flesh I shall see God, whom I myself shall see, and mine eyes shall behold, and not another.

Q. 212. What shall be the qualities or doweries of a glorified body?

A. Impassability, agility, clarity, subtility.

Q. 213. How do you prove its impassability, or incorruptibility?

A. Out of 1 Cor. xv. 53. For this corruptible must put on incorruption, and this mortal must put on immortality.

Q. 214. How prove you its agility?

A. Out of the same chapter, ver. 43, 44. It is sown in infirmity, it shall rise in power; it is sown a natural body, but it shall rise in a spiritual body, (that is, in motion, and some operations equal to a spirit;) which also proves its subtility.

Q. 215. How prove you it clarity?

A. Out of the same chapter, ver. 24 "For star (said he) differs from star in glory, so also the resurrection of the dead." And ver. 43. "It is sown in dishonour, it shall rise in glory."

Q. 216. In What space of time shall the dead rise, and the elect be thus changed?

A. "In a moment, in the twinkling of an eye," 1 Cor. xv, 52.

Q. 217. At What age and stature shall men rise?

A. At a perfect age, which is thirty-three, and in that stature which they should have had at a perfect age, without deformity by defect or excess.

Q. 218. How prove you this?

A. Out of Ephes. iv. 13. "The church shall last until we all meet into a perfect may, into the measure of the age of the fulness of Christ."

Q. 219. What example have you in nature for the resurrection?

A. A grain of corn, which first rots in the earth and then springs up and lives again.

Q. 220. What benefit have we by the knowledge of the resurrection?

A. It emboldens us to suffer persecution and death itself, in hope of future glory, according to that of St. Paul: "For sufferings of these times are not comparable to that of future glory, which be revealed in us:" Rom. viii. 18.

## The Twelfth Article

Q. 221. What is the twelfth article?

A. And life everlasting.

Q. 222. Why is this the last article?

A. Because everlasting life is the last end of man, and the last reward we expect by faith.

Q. 223. What understand you by this article?

A. I understand that such as keep the commandments, and die in the state of grace, shall live with God in bliss forever.

Q. 224. How prove you that keeping the commandments is of necessity for obtaining it?

A. Out of Matt. xix. 17, where Christ said to the young man, asking What he should do to obtain it, "If thou wilt enter into life, keep the commandments."

Q. 225. Is everlasting life given as a reward of our good works?

A. It is, according to Rom. ii. 6, 7. "God will render to every one according to his works, to them truly, that according to patience in good works, seek glory and honour, and incorruption life everlasting" &c.

Q. 226. Were all men created for everlasting life?

A. They were, for God "would have all men to be saved," 1 Tim. ii. 4. "He willeth not the death of any sinner, but rather that he be converted and live." Ezek. xxxiii. 11.

Q. 227. Why then are many damned?

A. By reason of their own wilful transgression of God's law, and final impenitence.

Q. 228. How prove you that man is the free cause of his own sin and damnation?

A. First out of Job xi. 23. "God (saith he) hath given him place for penance, but he abuseth it unto pride."

Secondly, out of Hos. xiii. 9. "The perdition is from thyself, O Israel; in me only is thy aid."

Thirdly, out of Rom. ii. 4. "The benignity of God calls thee to repentance, but thou heapest to thyself wrath and indignation, according to thy own impenitent heart."

Q. 229. In What consists everlasting life?

A. In the clear vision and fruition of God, according to that of our Saviour, in John xvii. 3. "This is the life everlasting, that they know thee the only true God, and Jesus Christ, whom thou hast sent."

Q. 230. Shall we see nothing in Heaven but God?

A. Yes, all the attributes and perfections of God, and in him also, as in a mirror or looking glass, the nature and perfections of all creatures; for he contains all things in himself in the most eminent manner.

Q. 231. How prove you that?

A. Out of the apostle, saying, "from whom all things by whom all things, and in whom all things." Rom xi. 36.

Q. 232. What effect will follow out the clear vision and fruition of God?

A. A divine love, steadfast possession and ineffable joy; and out of that praise, jubilation, and thanksgiving for ever.

Q. 233. What means the word Amen?

A. It means that the whole creed is divine truth, and therefore we most heartily assent to it.

## Hope and Prayer Explained

Q. 234. What is Hope?

A. It is a virtue infused by God into the soul, by which we have a confident expectation of glory to be obtained by the grace and merits of Christ, and our own merits proceeding from his grace.

Q. 235. On What is the confidence chiefly grounded?

A. On the merits and promises of Christ, who hath promised glory to such as hope in him, and do his works, as also grace whereby to do them.

Q. 236. Are our good works then meritorious of a reward of glory?

A. As proceeding from the grace of Christ, and built upon his promises, they are.

Q. 237. How prove you that?

A. First, out of Mark ix. 14. "For whosoever shall give you to drink a cup of water in my name because you are Christ's, Amen, I say to you, he shall not lose his reward."

Secondly, out of 1 Cor. iii. 8. "And every one shall receive his own reward, according to his own labour, for we are God's coadjutors."

Thirdly, out of Matt. v. 11. "Blessed are ye (saith our Lord) when they shall revile and persecute you; for very great is your reward in heaven."

Q. 238. Is it lawful for us to do good works in the hope of a reward?

A. Not only lawful but laudable, according to that, I "have inclined by heart, to do thy justifications for ever, for a reward." Psalm cxviii. 12.

Q. 239. What other proof have you?

A. Out of 1 John iii. 22. "Whatsoever (saith he) we shall ask of God, we shall receive of him, because we keep his commandments, and do those things that are pleasing before him."

Q. 240. How declare you the necessity of hope?

A. Because it produces in us obedience to the law of God, as also a willingness to suffer for his sake, and final perseverance.

Q. 241. How prove you that?

A. Out of Job xiii. 15. "Although he kill me, yet will I hope in him." And Psalm lv. 5. "In God have I hoped, I will not fear What flesh can do unto me."

It is according to the Psalmist, "Him that hopeth in our Lord, merely shall encompass." Psalm xxxi. 10.

And, "Our Lord is well pleased in them that hope in his mercy." Psalm cxlvi. 11.

Q. 242. What other good doth Hope?

A. It moves us to devout and humble prayer.

Q. 243. What is prayer?

A. It is the lifting up of the mind to God, by which we beg for good things and to be free
from evils, or by which we bless and praise God.

Q. 244. What are the conditions of good prayer?

A. That it may be made with reverence, attention, humility, and perseverance.

Q. 245. What vices are opposite to hope?

A. Despair and presumption.

Q. 246. What is despair?

A. It is a diffidence in the mercy of God, and merits of Christ, even to death.

Q. 247. What is presumption?

A. It is a foolish and desperate confidence of salvation, without endeavouring to live well or keep the commandments.

Q. 248. How is the despair the cause of sin?

A. Because despairing men are wont to say, if I shall be damned, I shall be damned, and so use no endeavour to do good or avoid evil.

Q. 249. How is presumption the cause of sin?

A. Because presumptuous men used to say, God is merciful and will forgive our sins,

How great soever, and at What time soever, we do penance; and out of this take liberty to sin.

Q. 250. How must our hope be balanced between these two extremes?

A. By a filial fear, and an humble distrust of our own works, as they are ours.

Q. 251. Is prayer good against both these?

A. It is, according to that of Luke xxii. 40, "pray ye that so ye may not fall into temptation."

Q. 252. For What else availeth prayer?

A. For the avoiding of evils and the obtaining all benefits.

Q. 253. How prove you that?

A. Out of John xv 23. "Whatsoever (saith our Saviour) ye shall ask my Father in my name, he will give it you." And Luke xi. 9. "Ask and it shall be given you," &c.

Q. 254. Is it lawful to pray in an unknown tongue?

A. It is, "for he that speaks in a tongue (unknown) speaks not to men but to God." 1 Cor. xiv. 2. And a petition has the same force if it be understood by him that is petitioned, whether the petitioner understood it or not.

Q. 255. What other proof have you?

A. Out of the same chap. ver. 16, 17, where Paul saith, "but if thou bless in spirit, (that is in a tongue not known) he that supplieth the place of the vulgar, How shall he say Amen, &c. thou indeed givest thanks well, but the other is not edified." You see in itself the thing is good, for he gives thanks well.

Q. 256. What means the apostle, when he exhorts us to pray always? Thess. v. 17.

A. He means we should daily spend some time to prayer, according to James v. 16. "Pray for one another that you may be saved, for the continual prayer of a just man availeth much."

Q. 257. Is it possible to pray always?

A. In some sense it is: namely, by offering up all our actions to God's honour.

Q. 258. In What place is prayer best?

A. In churches: because these are places consecrated and devoted to prayer, and there our prayers are elevated by the peculiar presence of God, and his special assistance besought by the Church's pastors in the consecration of those places.

Q. 259. How prove you that?

A. Out of Matt. xviii. 20. "Where there are two or three gathered together in my name (saith the Lord) there I am in the midst of them."

Q. 260. How prove you that material churches are of God's appointment?

A. First, Because God commanded Solomon to build him a temple, and dedicate it to his service. 2 Paral vii. 12.

Secondly, out of Luke xix. 46, where Christ calls the material temple his house, casing the buyers and sellers out of it. "My house, (saith he) is the house of prayer, but you have made it a den of thieves."

Thirdly, out of Luke xviii. 10, where the publican "ascended to the temple to pray, and descended into his house justified."

Q. 261. How do you prove it lawful to dedicate of consecrate material temples?

A. Out of Paralip. above cited, chap. 7, and out of John x. 22, where it is recorded that Christ himself kept the dedication of the temple in Jerusalem, instituted by Judas Maccabæus, 1 Mac. iv. 56, 59.

Q. 262. How do you prove it lawful to adorn the churches with tapestry, pictures, and the like?

A. Out of Mark, xiv. 15, where Christ commanded his last supper to be prepared in a great chamber adorned.

Q. 263. What proof have you for the order and number of the canonical hours?

A. For Matins, Lauds, and Prime, that of Psalm v. 4 "Early in the morning will I stand up to thee, early in the morning wilt thou hear my voice."

Q. 264. What for the third, sixth and ninth hours?

A. For the third out of Acts ii. 16. "At the third hour the Holy Ghost descended on the Apostles." For the sixth, out of Acts x. 9. "Peter and John went up into the higher part to pray about the sixth hour:" and for the ninth, out of Acts iii. 1. "And at the ninth hour Peter and John went up into the temple to pray."

Q. 265. What for the Even-song and Complin?

A. That of the Psalmist, "Morning and evening, will I declare the works of our Lord," Psalm liv. 18. and again, "lifting up of my hands is as an evening sacrifice," cxli 2.

Q. 266. Is it good to use outward ceremonies in a time of prayer, as kneeling, knocking the breast, and such like?

A. It is, for they declare the inward reverence and devotion of the heart; and Christ himself prostrated, when he prayed in the garden, Matt. xxvi. 39. And the poor publican beat his breast, and cast down his eyes in that prayer by which he merited to descend justified, Luke xviii. 13, 14.

Q. 267. Why is the morning so fit a time for prayer?

A. To open the windows of the soul to the light of divine grace and offer up the works of the whole day to God's honour.

Q. 268. Why is the evening also?

A. To shut the windows of the soul against the darkness of sin, and the illusions of the devil; as also to render thanks for all the benefits of the day past.

Q. 269. What things ought we to pray for?

A. For all good things both spiritual and temporal, and to be freed from evil; for so our Lord bath taught us by his prayer.

## The Lord's Prayer Expounded

Q. 270. What is the Pater Noster?

A. It is the most holy prayer, that ever was.

Q. 271. Who made it?

A. Christ our Lord, the eternal wisdom of his Father, Matt. vi. 9.

Q. 272. Why did he make it?

A. To teach us a set form of prayer, and How we ought to pray.

Q. 273. Why did he make it in so short and plain a manner?

A. That all persons might be able to understand and practise it.

Q. 274. What doth it contain?

A. All those chief things which we can ask or hope for of God.

Q. 275. How many petitions does it contain?

A. Seven.

Q. 276. What understand you by these words, which are prefixed to the petition, Our Father who art in Heaven?

A. I understand that God is our Father, both by creation and by adoption: and if we be in the state of grace, we may confidently come to him, and beg all blessings of him.

Q. 277. How prove you that?

A. Out of 1 John iii. 1. "See What manner of charity the Father hath given us, that we should be named, and be the sons of God."

Q. 278. Why do you say, our Father, and not my Father?

A. Because God is the common Father of all, and all good Christians must pray for one another, according to the article in the Creed. "I believe in the communion of saints."

Q. 279. What understand you by the words, Who art in heaven?

A. I understand that God who fills heaven and earth, and is in all things, times, and places, is in heaven in a peculiar manner, declaring and manifesting his glory to the blessed; and therefore when we pray, we must lift up our minds to him, and keep them fixed upon heavenly things.

Q. 280. How prove you that?

A. Out of Jer. xlviii. 10. "Cursed be he that doth the word of God negligently."

## The First Petition

Q. 281. What is the first petition?

A. Hallowed be thy name.

Q. 282. What do we beg by this?

A. That God may be known by the whole world, and that he may be worthily praised, served, and honoured by all his creatures, which cannot be effected but by his grace.

Q. 283. Who are these that say this petition ill?

A. Such as dishonour the name of God by blaspheming, swearing, lying, cursing, and scurrilous disclosures.

# The Second Petition

Q. 284. What is the second petition?

A. Thy kingdom come.

Q. 285. What do we beg of God by this petition?

A. We beg, that our miseries and afflictions in this life may be such, as that we may be made partakers of his joyful and heavenly kingdom hereafter.

Q. 286. What else do we beg?

A. That Christ may reign in us in this life by grace, and in the next by glory, presenting us a kingdom to his Father.

Q. 287. Who say this petition ill?

A. Such as are willing slaves to sin, and to the devil.

# The Third Petition

Q. 288. What is the third petition?

A. Thy will be done on earth as it is in heaven.

Q. 289. What do we beg by this?

A. That God would enable us by his holy grace to keep his commandments, and obey his will in all things.

Q. 290. What mean you by the words, on earth as it is in heaven?

A. We beg by those, that we may be as ready and willing to do the will of God on earth, as the blessed saints and angels are in heaven.

# The Fourth Petition

Q. 291. What is the fourth petition?

A. Give us this day our daily bread.

Q. 292. What do we beg by this?

A. All food and nourishment for our souls and bodies.

Q. 293. What is the food of the soul?

A. The word of God, the holy sacraments, especially the blessed Eucharist, and divine grace.

Q. 294. How prove you, that by this petition Christ intended the blessed bread of the Eucharist?

A. Because in Matt. vi. 11, we read "our supersubstantial bread."

Q. 295. Why is the Eucharist called our daily bread?

A. Because it is daily offered for our sins on the altar, and we ought daily to receive it, at least in spirit and desire.

Q. 296. Who say this petition ill?

A. Such as are cold and careless in coming to the sacraments, and in hearing divine service, or exhortations; and such as ascribe their temporal goods and blessings to their own industry and providence, and not to any special bounty or gift of God.

## The Fifth Petition

Q. 297. What is the fifth petition?

A. And forgive us our debts, as we forgive our debtors.

Q. 298. What do we beg by this petition?

A. That God would pardon us the sins of our life past, as also the punishments which are due unto them.

Q. 299. Why are sins, and the penalties of sin, called debts?

A. Because they make us debtors to the justice of God, whom by sin we rob of his due honour.

Q. 300. Why is it added, As we forgive our debtors?

A. To signify that God will not forgive us, unless we also forgive our brethren; "If you will not forgive men, neither will your Father forgive you your offences." Matt. vi. 15.

Q. 301. Who say this petition ill?

A. Such as bear malice against their neighbour, and seek revenge.

## The Sixth Petition

Q. 302. What is the sixth petition?

A. And lead us not into temptation.

Q. 303. What do we beg by this?

A. That God would not permit us to be tempted above our strength.

Q. 304. Doth God tempt any man to sin?

A. No, "God is not a tempter of evils, he tempts no man." James i. 13.

Q. 305. What other proof have you?

A. Out of Ps. v. 7 "Thou art not a God willing iniquity." And out of Rom. ix. 14. "Is there iniquity with God? No, God forbid."

Q. 306. By whom then are we tempted?

A. By the devil, and our own concupiscence.

Q. 307. Can a man live in this world, and be free from all temptations?

A. Morally speaking he cannot: "for the whole life of man on earth is a warfare." Job vii. 1.

Q. 308. Why then do we pray to be delivered from temptation?

A. That we may not be overcome, or vanquished by them.

Q. 309. Is temptation of itself a sin?

A. No, not without consent on our part; nay, it is a great occasion of merit, if we resist it as we ought.

Q. 310. How prove you that?

A. First, out of Apoc. ii. 10, 11. "Be thou faithful unto death (saith our Lord) and I will give thee the crown of life: he that overcometh, shall not be hurt by the second death."

Secondly, because Christ himself, who never sinned, would be tempted, "and the tempter came unto him." &c. Matt. iv. 3.

Q. 311. Are we never overcome by by our own default?

A. Never, according to that answer which was given to St. Paul, desiring to be freed from a temptation "My grace is sufficient for thee."

Q. 312. What other proof have you?

A. Out of James iv. 7. "Resist the devil, and he will flee from you."

Q. 313. Who are they that say this petition ill?

A. Such as seek after occasion of sin, and wilfully expose themselves unto temptations.

Q. 314. What are the best remedies against temptations?

A. To have recourse by humble prayer to God and to his saints, and to such especially as have undergone temptations of the same kind; to resist them valiantly at the first entrance, and to remember often the four last things, death, judgment, hell, and heaven.

## The Seventh Petition

Q. 315. What is the seventh petition?

A. But deliver us from evil.

Q. 316. What do we beg by this petition?

A. That God would deliver us from all our evils both spiritual and temporal, especially from the evils of sin past, present, and to come.

Q. 317. Who is the author of the evil sin?

A. The devil; for "Sin in God there is none." 1 John iii. 5.

Q. 318. What other proof have you?

A. Out of Wisdom xiv. 9. "Hateful to God is the impious man and his impiety."

Q. 319. Who say this petition ill?

A. They who commit their evils before God, and multiply their sins without remorse.

# The Hail Mary, or Angelical Salutation

Q. 320. What is the Hail Mary?

A. It is a most honourable salutation to the blessed Virgin Mary, and prayer to her.

Q. 321. How do your prove it lawful to honour her?

A. Out of Luke i. 48, where (by inspirations from God; she prophesied, saying, "All generations shall call me blessed."

Q. 322. How may parts hath the Hail Mary?

A. It hath three parts.

The First Part of the Hail Mary

Q. 323. What is the first part?

A. Hail Mary, full of grace, the Lord is with thee.

Q. 324. Who made this part?

A. The Holy Ghost, though it was delivered by the angel Gabriel, Luke i. 28.

Q. 325. What signifies the word Hail?

A. It signifies, Rejoice or be glad, O Mother of God.

Q. 326. Why do we invite her by this prayer to rejoice?

A. Because it renews the memory of her blessed Son's conception, which is an infinite

cause of joy to her and the whole court of heaven.

Q. 327. What signifies the word Mary?

A. It signifies star of the sea.

Q. 328. Why is she properly called the star of the sea?

A. Because she shines on us by her exemplary virtue in this sea of miseries, like a most glorious star.

Q. 329. What mean you by the words, full of grace?

A. I mean that the Blessed Virgin hath a special fulness and prerogative of grace for the conception of her Son.

Q. 330. What means, The Lord is with thee?

A. It means that the whole Trinity was with her at the time in a particular manner.

Q. 331. How declare you that?

A. Because the Father was with her, as with his Spouse, the Son as with his Mother, the Holy Ghost was with her, as with his choicest tabernacle.

Q. 332. Are they also now with her?

A. They are in glory, and will be so for all eternity.

## The Second Part of the Hail Mary

Q. 333. What is the second part of it?

A. Blessed art thou among women, blessed is the fruit of thy womb, JESUS.

Q. 334. Who made this part?

A. These words, Blessed art thou among women, were first delivered by the angel; and after with the rest, uttered by St. Elizabeth, being inspired by the Holy Ghost. Luke i. 28, 42.

Q. 335. What understand you by Blessed art thou among women?

A. I understand, she alone was chosen out amongst all women to be the Mother of God, and therefore ought to be blessed and praised by all women.

Q. 336. Why by married women?

A. Because their children are made the sons of God by the nativity and merits of her Son, of whom she daily also begs blessings for them.

Q. 337. Why by virgins?

A. Because she is their queen and chiefest patroness, and obtains for them of her Son Jesus, the gift of chastity.

Q. 338. Why by widows?

A. Because she is their best example, and advocate to their Spouse, her Son.

Q. 339. What means, Blessed is the fruit of thy womb, Jesus?

A. It means, that Jesus is her true and natural Son, and in him she is the author of all our blessings, and to be blessed both by men and angels.

Q. 340. Why are Catholics such great honourers of the name Jesus.

A. Because it is a name above all names, as you have heard in the creed; and as St. Paul exhorts, saying "all Whatsoever you do in word or work, do all in the name of our Lord Jesus Christ, giving thanks to God the Father by him." Colos. iii. 17.

## The Third Part of the Hail Mary

Q. 341. What is the third part of the Hail Mary?

A. Holy Mary, Mother of God, pray for us sinners, now, and in the hour of our death.

Amen.

Q. 342. Who made this part?

A. The holy Catholic Church in the Council of Ephesus, the year of our Lord 431, (Pope Celestine presiding,) against Nestorius, the heretic, who denied our blessed Lady to be the Mother of God, and would only have her called the Mother of Christ. See Baronius, tom. 5. An. 4. 31.

Q. 343. What means, Pray for us sinners now?

A. It means, that we need divine assistance every moment.

Q. 344. What means, And at the hour of our death?

A. It meaneth that we then especially shall need the aid of the blessed Mary, and her Son Jesus, and therefore do daily beg it. The word Amen, signifies, let it be done, or be it so.

# Charity Expounded

Q. 345. What is Charity?

A. It is the gift of God, or a supernatural quality infused by God into the soul of man, by which we love God above all things, and our neighbours as ourselves, for God's sake.

Q. 346. Why is it called supernatural?

A. Because it is not in the power of nature to obtain it, but by the special grace and gift of God.

Q. 347. Is charity imputed as protestants would have it, or is it a quality truly inherent in the soul.

A. It is truly inherent in the soul, as wisdom is inherent in a soul that is wise, and love in a soul that loves.

Q. 348. How prove you that?

A. First out of Rom. v. 5. "The charity of God which is poured forth in our hearts, by the Holy Ghost, which is given us."

Secondly, out of Dan. vi, 22, "Before him (i.e. God) justice have been found in me."

Thirdly, out of Ephes. iii. 17, 18, where St. Paul prays for his brethren, "That Christ may dwell by faith in your hearts: that, being rooted and founded in charity, you may be able to comprehend, with all the saints, What is the breadth, and length, and height, and depth."

Q. 349. What is it to love God above all things?

A. To be willing to lose all things, rather than the grace or love of God by mortal sin.

Q. 350. Who has this love?

A. They who keep the commandments of God, according to that, "This is the charity of God, that we keep his commandments; and his commandments are not heavy." 1 John v. 3.

Q. 351. Hath not he charity then, that breaks any of the commandments?

A. He hath not; for "he that saith, he knoweth God, and doth not keep his commandments, is a liar, and the truth is not in him." 1 John ii. 4.

Q. 352. What is it to love our neighbours as ourselves?

A. To wish him as much good as we wish ourselves, and to do him no wrong.

Q. 353. Who is our neighbour?

A. All men, women, and children, even those who injure us, or differ from us in religion, but especially Catholics.

Q. 354. Why so?

A. Because they are the images of God, and redeemed with the blood of Christ.

Q. 355. Why especially Catholics?

A. Because they are all members of the mystical body of Christ, which is the church.

Q. 356. Whence ariseth the obligations of loving our neighbour?

A. Because God hath commanded it: and 'if one shall say I love God, and hateth his brother, he is a liar.' 1 John, iv. 20.

Q. 357. Are we not also bound to love our enemies?

A. We are, according to that, "It was said of old, Thou shalt not kill: but I say unto you, Love your enemies." Matt. v. 43, 44.

Q. 358. What kind of love are we bound to show to our enemies?

A. We are bound to use a civil behaviour towards them, to pray for them in general, and to be disposed to do any charitable office for them when their necessity require it.

Q. 359. What is the highest act of charity?

A. To give our life for God's honour, and the salvation of our neighbour.

Q. 360. Why is charity the greatest and most excellent of virtues?

A. Because it is the life of all the rest. "Faith without charity is dead." James ii. 26.

Q. 361. What state of life do we conceive to be of greatest perfection.

A. That which of its own nature and proper institution obligeth to the highest and greatest charity, for charity is perfection, and such is the state not only of bishops, but also, as many probably think, of pastors who have the charge of souls.

Q. 362. How prove you that?

A. Out of 1 John xv. 13; "Greater charity than this no man hath, that a man yield his life for his friends," which is the proper obligation of every parish priest, according to that, "The good pastor giveth his life for his sheep." John x. 12.

Q. 363. How prove you the necessity of charity?

A. Out of John iv. 16. "He that remains in charity, remains in God, and God in him," and chap. iii. ver 14, "He that loves not, remains in death."

Q. 364. What are the effects of charity?

A. It destroys sin. "Charity covers a multitude of sins," James v. 20, and gives spiritual life to the soul. "In this we know that we are translated from death to life, because we love the brethren." 1 John iii. 14.

# Of the Commandments in general

Q. 365. What is the principal aim or end of the commandments?

A. To teach us the will and pleasure of the eternal God, or the love of God, and our

neighbour. "He that loveth his neighbour hath fulfilled the law." Rom. xiii. 8.

Q. 366. Why are the commandments (excepting the determination of the sabbath

day) called the commandments of the law of nature?

A. Because God wrote them in the heart of men at the creation, being the very dictates of
natural reason.

Q. 367. When did he renew them in the written law?

A. When he gave them to Moses on mount Sinai, in thunder and lightening, written in two tables of stone Exod. xx.

Q. 368. Why in thunder and lightening?

A. To move us to a careful observance of them.

Q. 369. Are all men bound to know the commandments?

A. For the substance of them they are, because they are the rule of our whole life and actions.

Q. 370. How do you prove them to be only ten?

A. Out of Deut. iv. 13, "He shewed his covenant which he commanded you to do, and the ten words which be wrote in two tables of stone."

Q. 371. By What kind of sins are the commandments broken?

A. By mortal sins only; for venial sins are not strictly speaking contrary to the end of the commandments, which is charity.

Q. 372. How declare you that?

A. Because a venial sin, for example, a vain word, an officious or jesting lie, which hurts nobody, the theft of a pin or an apple, is not of weight enough to break charity between man and man, much less between God and man.

Q. 373. Is it possible for us to keep all the commandments?

A. Not only possible, but necessary and easy, by the assistance of God's grace.

Q. 374. How do you prove that?

A. Because God is not a tyrant to command impossibilities under pain of eternal damnation, as he doth the keeping his commandments.

Q. 375. How prove you that?

A. First out of Exod. xx. and Deut. xxviii. 15. where he often commands them to be kept, threatening grievous punishments to such as break them.

Secondly, out of Matt. v. 19. "Whosoever, therefore, shall break one of these least commandments, and shall teach men so, he shall be called the least in the kingdom of heaven: but whosoever shall do and teach the same shall be called great in the kingdom of heaven."

Thirdly, out of Matt. xi. 29, 30. "Take up my yoke upon you (saith the Lord) for my yoke is sweet, and my burden light." And again, 1 John v. 3. "His commandments are not heavy."

Q. 376. Hath God ever promised to enable man to keep them?

A. He hath, and also actually to make them keep and do them.

Q. 377. How prove you that?

A. Out of Ezek. xxxvi. 27. "I will put my spirit in the middle of you, (said our Lord) and I will make ye walk in my precepts, and keep my judgments and do them." And again, chap. xxxvii. 23, 24. "They shall be my people, and I will be their God, there shall be one pastor of them all, and they shall walk in my judgments and keep my commandments and do them.

Q. 378. How do you prove that any have kept them?

A. Out of Luke i. 6. "Zachary and Elizabeth were both just before God: walking in all the commandments and justifications of our Lord without reproof."

Q. 379. How prove you the keeping of them to be necessary to salvation?

A. First, out of Matt. xix. 17. "If thou wilt enter into life (saith our Lord) keep the commandments."

Secondly, out of Luke x. 25, 28, where the lawyer had asked, What he should do to possess everlasting life, and had repeated the sum of the commandments:

58

Christ answered him saying, "Do this, and thou shalt live."

Thirdly, out of Rom. ii. 13, "Not hearers of the law are just with God, but the doers of the law shall be justified."

# OF THE COMMANDMENTS IN PARTICULAR

## The First Commandment Expounded

Q. 380. What is the first commandment?

A. I am the Lord thy God, who brought thee out of the land of Egypt, and out of the house of bondage. Thou shalt not have strange gods before me. Thou shalt not make to thyself a graven thing, nor the likeness of any thing that is in heaven above, or in the earth below, or of those things that are in the waters under the earth. Thou shalt not adore nor worship them; I am the Lord thy God, mighty, jealous, visiting the sins of the fathersupon their children, to the third and fourth generation of them that hate me; and showing mercy to thousands of those that love me, and keep my commandments. Exod. xx.

Q. 381. What are we commanded by this precept?

A. To serve, love, adore, and worship one only, true, living, and eternal God, and no
more.

Q. 382. What are we forbidden by this precept?

A. Not to worship any creature for a God, or give to it the honour which is due to God.

Q. 383. What is the honour due to God?

A. A supreme and sovereign honour, which is called by divines Latria; by which we honour him as the great master of life and death, as our creator, redeemer, preserver, and last end.

Q. 384. How do men sin against this commandment?

A. By worshipping idols and false gods, by erring or doubting in faith, by superstition and witchcraft.

Q. 385. How else?

A. By communicating with infidels or heretics, by believing dreams, &c.

Q. 386. How do you prove it a great sin to go to church with heretics?

A. Because by so doing we outwardly deny our faith, and profess their false faith.

Q. 387. What scripture have you against it?

A. Out of Luke xvii. 23, 24, where Christ forbids it, saying, "And they shall say unto you, Lo! here is Christ, Lo, there Christ; go ye not, neither do you follow them."

Q. 388. What other proof have you?

A. Out of Tit. iii. 10, 11. "A man that is a heretic, after the first and second admonition, avoid, knowing that he that is such an one is subverted and sinneth."

Q. 389. How do you prove it unlawful to go to witches and fortune-tellers?

A. Out of Deut. xviii. 10, 11. "There shall not be found among you any one that shall expiate his son or daughter making them to pass through the fire, or that useth divination, or any observer of times, or enchanter, or witch, or a charmer, or a wizard, or necromancer, &c. For all these things our Lord abhorreth."

Q. 390. What understand you by these words. Thou shalt not make to thyself any graven thing, &c. Thou shalt not adore them, &c.

A. I understand that we must not make idols or images, nor any graven thing Whatsoever, to adore it as a god, or with God's honour.

Q. 391. Why are not these words expressed at length in many of our short catechisms?

A. Because they are sufficiently included in the preceding words, "Thou shalt not have strange (or other) gods before me."

Q. 392. How declare you that?

A. Because if we must have no other but the only true God, who created heaven and earth, then it is clear to the reason of every child, that we must not have many gods, or any graven things for gods, or adore any other things for God.

Q. 393. Why do Protestants of those of new religions, instead of graven things, translate graven images?

A. Because they have a will to corrupt the text, in hope by so doing to persuade ignorant people, that Catholics are idolaters, and break the first commandment by making and worshipping images.

Q. 394. How do you prove they corrupt the text?

A. Because the Hebrew word is Pesel, which signifies a graven thing, the Greek is Idolon, and the Latin is Sculptile, a graven thing; therefore the word Image is a mere corruption.

Q. 395. Is it lawful then to give any honour to the images of Christ and his saints?

A. Yes, an inferior or relative honour, as much as they represent unto us heavenly things, but not God's honour, nor yet the honour due the saints.

Q. 396. How prove you that?

A. Out of Exod. xxv. 18, 19, 22, where God himself commanded "two cherubims to be made of beaten gold, and to be set on both sides of the ark (before which the people were to pray) and promised that he would speak unto them from the middle of the cherubims;" therefore it is lawful to make images and pray before them.

Q. 397. Do not Catholics pray to images and relics?

A. By no means; we pray before them, indeed, to excite our devotion, and to keep our thoughts collected upon heavenly subjects; but we do not, at all, pray to them; for we know well they can neither see, nor hear, nor help us.

Q. 398. What other proof have you for the lawful use of images?

A. First, out of John iii. 14, where Christ approves the making and exalting the brazen serpent, by which the Israelites were healed in the desert, and owns it to be an image or figure of himself, exalted on the cross.

Secondly, because we read in Baronius, that the famous church historian, in the year of Christ, 31, that Christ himself sent his own image to king Abdagar, and made it also by the miracle on the handkerchief of St. Veronica, and on his own shroud. Add to this, the second Nicene council, Actio 4, anathematizes image-breakers, that is such as shall break them in contempt or scorn, and all such as allege the places in scripture, which are against idols, are against the sacred images; and also those who say that Catholics honour images as God, with sovereign honour.

Q. 399. How could you further satisfy a Protestant, that should charge you with idolatry, in giving sovereign honour to pictures and images?

A. I would for satisfaction herein, if necessary, break a crucifix, or tear a picture of Jesus Christ in pieces, and throw the pieces into the fire; and would show him the council of Trent, Sess. 25, which teaches thus, "Images are not to be venerated for any virtue of divinity that is believed to be in them, or for any trust or confidence that is to be put in them, as the Gentiles did of old, who reposed their hope and trust in their idols; but because the honour that is exhibited to them, is referred to the prototypes represented by them" &c.

Q. 400. What benefits do we receive by images?

A. Very great, because they movingly represent to us the mysteries of our Saviour's passion, as also by martyrdoms and examples of his saints.

Q. 401. Is there not some danger of Idolatry in the frequent use of idols?

A. Truely none at all; for it is not possible that any rational man, who is instructed in Christianity, would conceive or think a piece of painted wood or marble, is that God and man, Jesus Christ, who was born of the Virgin Mary, died on the cross, arose from the dead, ascended into heaven, and sits now on the right hand of God.

Q. 402. But How, if such inconveniences happen, at least by accident?

A. Let the abuse be mended, and not the good institution taken away or blamed; For man's nature is subject to hurt itself, even in the best things, which must not therefore be given over.

Q. 403. How do you prove it lawful to paint God the Father like an old man, seeing he is pure spirit, and hath no body?

A. Because he appeared to the prophet Daniel in the shape of an old man, Dan. 7, but this is to be understood, that the pictures we make, are not the proper images of God the Father, but the shape wherein he appeared to Daniel. And the like is to be understood of the pictures of angels, to wit, that they are not proper images of them, according to their spiritual substance, but of the shape they appear in to men.

Q. 404. What utility doth accrue to us by our honouring and canonizing Saints?

A. Very great, seeing it much conduceth to the imitation of their virtues, and the love of God, making us know that it is possible even for ourselves, to come to the like reward.

Q. 405. How declare you that?

A. Because the higher esteem we have of the saints, and the excellency of their state, the more ardent must needs be our desire, and the stronger our courage, to do and undertake What they did and practised.

Q. 406. Is it lawful to honour the angels and saints?

A. It is with Dulia, an inferior honour, proportioned to their excellency, which they have from God; it is God we honour in them.

Q. 407. How prove you that?

A. First, out of Josue v. 14, where the angel of the Lord said to Josue, "I am the prince of the host of our Lord." Josue fell on his face to the ground; and worshipping said, "What saith my Lord to his servant?"

Secondly, out of Apoc. xxii. 8, where John (though the angel had already forbidden him so to do, because of his apostolical dignity, chap xix. 10.) "fell down to adore before the feet of the angel, who shewed him these things."

Q. 408. Is it lawful to honour the relics of saints?

A. With a relative honour it is, referring it to God's honour.

Q. 409. How prove you that?

A. First, because a dead man was raised from death to life by touching the bones of Eliseus the prophet, 4 Kings xiii. 21.

Secondly, out of Matt. ix. 20, 21, where we read the woman was healed of her bloody flux, but by the touching the hem of our Saviour's garment, and believing it would heal her.

Thirdly, out of Acts xviii. 19. "The handkerchiefs and aprons which had but touched the body of St. Paul, cast out devils, and cured all diseases."

Q. 410. How prove you that dead and inanimate things, (for example, medals, crosses, churches, bread, water and the like) are capable of sanctity and honour?

A. First, out of Joshua iv. 16, and Exod. iii. 5, where the Angel saith to Moses and Joshua, "Loose thy shoes from 'thy feet, for the ground whereon thou standest is holy ground."

Secondly, out of Matt. xxiii. 17, 18, where we read, that the temple sanctifieth the gold, and the altar the gift. "Ye fools and blind, (saith our Lord,) whether is greater, the gold, or the temple that sanctifieth the gold? the gift, or the altar that sanctifieth the gift?

Thirdly, out of Tim. iv. 4, 5. "Every creature of God is sanctified by the word of God and prayer," and out of

2 Peter i. 18, where he calls the mountain Tabor a holy hill, because Christ was transfigured upon it.

Q. 411. How prove you that pilgrimages to holy places, as to mount Calvary, mount Tabor, and the sepulchre of Christ, are laudable and pious practices?

A. First, out of Deut. xvi. 16, where God himself commanded, that thrice a year all the people should come up into Jerusalem, to adore and make their offerings to him."

Secondly, the example of Christ himself, our blessed Lady, and St. Joseph, "who went up to Jerusalem, the solemn day of the Pasch." Luke ii. 41, 42.

Thirdly, out of Acts viii. where the Ethiopian eunuch, going on a pilgrimage to Jerusalem, was in his return converted and baptized by St. Philip, so pleasing was his pilgrimage to God.

Finally, because it was foretold by the prophets that these places which Christ sanctified by his passion should be of great pilgrimage and adoration, "We will adore (saith David) in the place where his feet stood," Psalm cxxxi. 7. And in Isa. xi. 10, we read, "To him shall the Gentiles pray, and his sepulchre shall be glorious."

Q. 412. How do you prove it lawful to go on pilgrimages to the shrines of Saints?

A. Because, as you have read already, their relics are holy and venerable things, and God is pleased to work great cures and miracles by them for such as are devout honourers of them.

Q. 413. If there any power now in the church to do miracles?

A. There is according to that unlimited promise of Christ. "And these signs shall follow them that believe: In my name they shall cast out devils; they shall speak with new tongues: they shall lay their hands upon the sick, and they shall recover." Mark xvi. 17.

Q. 414. Have these things been done in latter ages?

A. They have, and are, as you may see in the unquestioned histories and records of all Catholic countries; where many great miracles wrought by the servants of God, especially at pilgrimages and shrines of Saints, are yearly registered under the depositions of eye-witnesses, men above all exceptions, which cannot be denied unless we deny all history.

Q. 415. Why do the pretended reformers say miracles are ceased?

A. Because they have never yet been able to do any in confirmation of their errors.

Q. 416. Why are so few done here in our days?

A. By reason of incredulity of many bad Christians. Matt. xiii. 58.

Q. 417. What necessity is there for the belief of miracles?

A. Doubtless very great; because the belief of miracles well grounded, make men extremely apprehensive of the presence of God, and his immediate government of human affairs; so that he who absolutely denies miracles, is to be suspected of not believing particular providence, which is the main string on which all Christianity depends.

# The Second Commandment Expounded

Q. 418. What is the second commandment?

A. Thou shalt not take the name of the Lord by God in vain.

Q. 419. What is forbidden by this precept.

A. All false, rash, and unnecessary oaths.

Q. 420. What kind of sins are false and rash oaths?

A. Mortal sins, if they be voluntary and deliberate, because by such oaths, we call God to

witness a lie; or at least to that which is uncertain.

Q. 421. What are the necessary conditions of a lawful oath?

A. Truth, that we hurt not God's honour; justice that we wrong not our neighbour; and judgment, that we swear not vainly.

Q. 422. What is the just cause of an oath?

A. God's honour, our own, or our neighbour's good and defence.

Q. 423. If a man swears to do that which is evil, is he bound to keep his oath?

A. No, he is not bound to keep it; for an oath is no bond of iniquity.

Q. 424. How prove you a vain or jesting oath to be a sin?

A. Out of Matt. v. 33. "It was said of old (saith our Lord) Thou shalt not commit perjury; but I say unto you, not to swear at all," that is without just cause.

Q. 425. What other proof have you?

A. Out of James v. 12. "But above all things, my brethren, swear not, neither by heaven, nor by earth, nor by any other oath. But let your speech be: Yea, yea: no, no: that you fall not under judgment."

Q. 426. What else is prohibited by this precept?

A. All cursing and blaspheming.

Q. 427. How else do men sin against this precept?

A. By breaking lawful vows, and by making or keeping unlawful ones.

Q. 428. What is a lawful vow?

A. It is a deliberate and voluntary promise made to God, of some better good.

Q. 429. How do you prove it lawful to make vows?

A. Out of Isa. xix. 21. "They shall make vows unto the Lord, and shall pay them."

Q. 430. What is commanded by this precept?

A. To speak always with reverence of God, and his saints.

# The Third Commandment Expounded

Q. 431. What is the third commandment?

A. Remember that thou keepest holy the sabbath day.

Q. 432. When did the Sabbath begin to be kept?

A. From the very creation of the world; for then God blessed the seventh day, and rested on it from all His works. Gen. ii. 2.

Q. 433. When was this commandment renewed?

A. In the Old Law; when God gave the commandments to Moses on mount Sinai, written with His own finger in two tables of stone, Exod. xx. 1, &c. xxxi. 18.

Q. 434. Why was the Jewish Sabbath changed into the Sunday?

A. Because Christ was born upon a Sunday, arose from the dead upon a Sunday, and sent down the Holy Ghost on a Sunday: works not inferior to the creation of the world.

Q. 435. By whom was it changed?

A. By the Governors of the Church, the Apostles, who also kept it; for St. John was in spirit on the Lord's day (which was Sunday.) Apoc. i. 10.

Q. 436. How prove you that the Church hath power to command feasts and holydays?

A. By the very act of changing the sabbath into Sunday, which Protestants allow of; and therefore they fondly contradict themselves, by keeping Sunday strictly, and breaking most other feasts commanded by the same Church.

Q. 437. How prove you that?

A. Because by keeping Sunday, they acknowledge the Church's power to ordain feasts, and to command them under sin; and by not keeping the rest by her commanded, they again deny, in fact, the same power.

Q. 438. What other proof have you?

A. Out of John x. 22, where we read that Christ himself was present, and kept the Dedication of the temple in Jerusalem, a feast ordained by Judas Maccabæus, 1 Macc. Iv And out of Acts ii. 1, 4, where the Apostles, keeping the feast of Pentecost, "were all filled with the Holy Ghost." Neither do Protestants as yet differ from this, though some have lately prohibited and profaned both it and the holy feast of the Resurrection, and all the other feasts of the Church.

Q. 439. What commandment have you from God for obedience to the Church in things of this nature?

A. Out of Acts xv. 41, where we read that "St. Paul went about confirming the Churches, and commanding them to keep the precepts of the Apostles and the ancients." And out of Luke x. 16, "He that heareth you, heareth me; and he that despiseth you (the Church) despiseth me."

Q. 440. May temporal princes and the laity make a holy day?

A. With consent and approbation of the Church, they may, otherwise not; because this is an act of spiritual jurisdiction.

Q. 441. For What end doth the Church ordain holydays?

A. For the increase of piety, and the memory of special benefits received from God.

Q. 442. If keeping the Sunday be a church precept, Why is it numbered in the decalogue, which are the Commandments of God, and the Law of Nature?

A. Because the substance or chief part of it, namely Divine Right, and the Law of Nature; though the determining this particular day, Sunday rather than Saturday, be a Church ordinance and precept.

Q. 443. Did not Christ, when he confirmed the rest, confirm also this commandment?

A. In as much as it belongeth to the law of nature, he did: but not as it belonged to the ceremonial law of the Jews, and was affixed to Saturday, therefore, now we are not bound to keep Saturday.

Q. 444. Why so, I pray you?

A. Because that particular day was a command of the ceremonial law of the Jews, which was abrogated, and ceased to oblige after the death of Christ.

Q. 445. To What are we obliged by this precept?

A. To spend Sunday in prayer and divine service.

Q. 446. What is the best means to sanctify the Sunday?

A. By hearing mass, confessing our sins, communicating, hearing sermons, and reading good books.

Q. 447. What is forbidden by this precept?

A. All profane employments, and servile labours, excepting such as are of necessity, as dressing meat, serving cattle, &c. or such as appertain to piety and works of mercy.

Q. 448. Who break this commandment?

A. Such as without necessity spend any considerable part of the Sunday in servile labours.

Q. 449. How else is the Sunday profaned?

A. By spending all the morning slothfully in bed, or vainly dressing ourselves; by missing divine service when we may hear it, or spending a part of the day in drinking, gaming, dancing, or the like.

Q. 450. Is there any thing now in this first table of the law impossible to be observed?

A. No certainly; for nothing can be more easy and delightful to the true servant of God, than the things that are here commanded.

Q. 451. Why do you now divide the table of Moral law into three and seven, whereas anciently some Fathers assigned four to the first table, and six to the last?

A. Concerning the manner of limiting the number of commandments to each table, the scripture says nothing, not so much as which is the third, which is the fourth commandment, and therefore it is in itself indifferent: St. Jerome divides them into four and six, which is no where condemned, St. Augustine into three and seven, who is more generally followed; but indeed the matter is of no great importance How we reckon them so we retain them in our books, and keep them in our lives.

Q. 452. But What reason can justify the omission of so great a part of the text, when we transcribe the commandments into our catechisms?

A. Such books being composed principally for the unlearned, are by the pastors of the church abridged into the shortest and easiest method they can, prudently condescending to the weak memories and low capacities of the people: nor can the church be accused of the least shadow of corrupting or omitting any part of the commandments, or of God's word; since in no Catholic Bible is there one syllable left out; and whether the first commandment, after this account, be divided, and the two last united, or contrawise the last divided and the first united, is not at all material, the whole ten commandments being entirely contained in both, or either way.

# THE SECOND TABLE OF THE LAW

## The Fourth Commandment Expounded

Q. 453. What is the fourth commandment?

A. Honour thy father and mother.

Q. 454. What are we commanded by this precept.

A. To love, reverence, obey, and relieve our parents in their wants.

Q. 455. Why to love them?

A. Because, under God they are the chief causes of our very life and being; and do not only bring us up with much love, labour, and solicitude.

Q. 456. How are we bound to reverence them?

A. Not only inwardly in our heart, but also outwardly in our carriage and comportment.

Q. 457. Why to obey them?

A. Because they are God's vicegerents, and have received power from him (from whom is all paternity in heaven and earth) both to direct us, instruct us, and correct us.

Q. 458. In What things are we bound to obey our parents?

A. In all that is not sin, according to that, "Children obey your parents in all things, for that is pleasing unto God." Col. iii. 20.

Q. 459. What is prohibited by the precept?

A. All sourness, stubborness, and disobedience to parents.

Q. 460. What is the reward of dutiful children?

A. Long and happy life; "The blessing of heaven comes upon them, and remains to the end of their days." Eccl. iii. 10.

Q. 461. What is the reward of undutiful children?

A. A short and sinful life, accompanied with an untimely death witness the example of Absalom, 2 Kings viii. 14.

Q. 462. What other proof have you?

A. That of Prov. xxx. 17. "The eye that mocketh at his father, and that despiseth the travail of his mother in bearing him, let the ravens of the torrent pick it out and the young of the eagle eat it."

Q. 463. What signifies the word Father?

A. It signifies not only our corporal parents, but also our Ghostly Father, and all lawful superiors.

Q. 464. What owe we to the Ghostly Father?

A. Love, reverence, obedience, and maintenance.

Q. 465. Why love?

A. Because they are the fathers and feeders of our souls, and under God and his saints, the instrumental causes of our spiritual good: "For in Christ Jesus I have begotten you through the gospel," (saith St. Paul) 1 Cor. iv. 15.

Q. 466. Why reverence?

A. Because they are God's anointed, and represent the person of Christ.

Q. 467. Why obedience?

A. Because God hath appointed them to be our spiritual pastors, guides, and governors.

Q. 468. In What are we bound to obey them?

A. In all things belonging to faith, doctrine, and the government of our souls.

Q. 469. Is any great honour due to priests and ghostly fathers?

A. There is, according to that of St. Paul. "Let the priests who rule well be esteemed worthy of double honour; especially they who labour in the word and doctrine." 1 Tim. v. 17.

Q. 470. Have you any other place?

A. Yes, Eccle. vii. 13, 32, 33, "With all thy soul fear our Lord and reverence his priests, with all thy strength, love them that made thee and forsake not his master, honour God with all thy soul, and honour the priests." And the reason is, for if we owe love, honour, and obedience to our carnal parents, much more to our spiritual, by How much the soul surpasseth the body. Again, as there is none greater than priests, who are empowered to shut and open the gates of heaven, as also to convert the substance of bread and wine, into the most precious body and blood of our blessed Saviour: to no person is greater honour due, than to them who personate Christ himself, so that he who despiseth them despiseth Christ himself, and the disregard of them is the origin of impiety.

Q. 471. How may we sin against priests and ghostly fathers?

A. By disobeying or detracting them, or believing slanderous reports against them, upon mere hearsay, or the testimony of insufficient witnesses, or without witnesses.

Q. 472. What testimony is sufficient against a priest?

A. I will tell you out of St. Paul's mouth: "Against a priest (saith he to Timothy the bishop of Ephesus) receive not an accusation under two or three witnesses." 1 Tim. v. 19, and 21, "I charge thee before God, and Christ Jesus, and the elect angels, that thou observe these things without prejudice, doing nothing by declining to either side."

Q. 473. Is it convenient to ask a blessing of priests?

A. It is, because they give it in the name and person of Christ.

Q. 474. What warrant have you for it?

A. First out of Mark 14, 16, where "Christ laying his hands upon the children, blessed them."

Secondly, the example of Melchisedech blessing Abraham; upon which St. Paul saith, "without all contradiction, that which is less, is blessed of the better." Heb. vii. 7.

Q. 475. What scripture have you for obedience to priests?

A. Heb. xiii. 17. "Obey your prelates, and be subject to them; for they watch, as being to render an account for your souls." And in the old law, disobedience to the priests was punished with death, Deut. xvii. 12.

Q. 476. In What are we bound under sin to obey princes and temporal magistrates?

A. In all things (which are not sin) belonging to the good and peace of the commonwealth.

Q. 477. How prove you that?

A. First, out of Rom. xiii. 1. "Let every soul be subject to the higher powers, for there is no power but of God: he therefore that resists power, resists the ordinance of God." Secondly, out of 1 Pet. ii. 13, 14. "Be ye subject to every creature for God, whether to the king as excelling, or to magistrates, as sent by him to the revenge of malefactors.

Q. 478. What if kings or magistrates command us to do sin, or things against our conscience?

A. Then we must answer them with the apostles, 'we must obey God, rather than men." Acts v. 29.

Q. 479. In What are servants bound to obey their masters?

A. In all things that are not sin, belonging to their charge.

Q. 480. How prove you that?

A. Out of Coloss. iii. 22. "Servants, obey in all things your masters, according to the flesh, not serving the eye, as pleasing men, but in simplicity of heart, as pleasing God.

Q. 481. How do servants sin against their masters?

A. By neglecting their commands, stealing or spoiling their goods, &c.

## The Fifth Commandment Expounded

Q. 482. What is the fifth commandment?

A. Thou shalt not kill.

Q. 483. What is prohibited by this?

A. All murder, unjust shedding of blood, fighting and quarreling.

Q. 484. Is it not lawful to kill in any cause?

A. Yes, in a just war, or when public justice requires it: "For the magistrate beareth not the sword without cause." Rom. i. 4. As also in the blameless defence of our own, or our innocent neighbour's life, against an unjust invader.

Q. 485. Is it lawful to fight duels, appointing a set time and place, for private interest, or punctilios of honour?

A. No, by no means; for the church hath forbidden it under excommunication, to be incurred ipso facto; and such as die in duels, can be neither have Christian burial nor be prayed for the church.

Q. 486. How prove you all fighting and quarreling to be unlawful?

A. Out of Matt. v. 39. "You have heard (saith Christ) it was said of old, and eye for an eye, and a tooth for a tooth; but I say unto you not to resist evil, but if any other strike thee on the right cheek, turn to him also the other."

Q. 487. What else is forbidden by this precept?

A. To seek, wish, or desire our own, or any other man's death, out of impatience or passion, or to cause women with child to miscarry.

# The Sixth Commandment Expounded

Q. 488. What is the sixth commandment?

A. Thou shalt not commit adultery.

Q. 489. What is prohibited by this precept?

A. All carnal sin with another man's wife, or another woman's husband, and chiefly adultery; as also fornication and pollution.

Q. 490. How prove you fornication and pollution to be mortal sins?

A. Out of Col. iii. 5, 6. "Mortify, therefore, (saith St. Paul,) your members, which are upon earth: fornication, uncleaness, lust, evil concupiscence, and covetousness, which is the service of idols: for which things the wrath of God cometh upon the children of unbelief."

Q. 491. In What case is it lawful for a man to dismiss his wife?

A. Only in case of evident adultery.

Q. 492. Can he that hath so dismissed his wife, marry another during her life?

A. He cannot; for "he that dismisseth his wife and marries another, committeth adultery." Matt. v. 32. And Luke xvi. 18. "He that marries her, that is so dismissed, commits adultery."

Q. 493. Why is adultery a far greater sin than fornication?

A. Because it is a greater injury to our innocent neighbour, as also to the sacrament of matrimony.

Q. 494. How prove you that a wife so dismissed from her husband, cannot marry again during her husband's life?

A. Out of 1 Cor. vii. 10, 11. "But to them, that are married, not I, but the Lord commandeth, that the wife depart not from her husband: and if she depart, that she remain unmarried." And ver. 39. "A woman is bound to the law, so long as her husband liveth; but if her husband sleep (that is be dead) she is at liberty, let her marry whom she will."

Q. 495. What else is forbidden by this precept?

A. Whoredom, incest, sacrilege, and sins against nature.

Q. 496. Why is lust hateful in the sight of God?

A. Because it defiles in us the image of God, and the temple of the Holy Ghost.

Q. 497. What more is here prohibited?

A. Unchaste touching of ourselves or others, with delight in lustful thoughts and kisses.

Q. 498. What is the heir of unlawful lust?

A. Death and damnation; for, "neither fornicators nor adulterers, nor effeminate," (that is such as defile themselves with voluntary pollution,) "shall possess the kingdom of God." 1 Cor. vi. 9.

# The Seventh Commandment Expounded

Q. 499. What is the seventh commandment?

A. Thou shalt not steal.

Q. 500. What is forbidden by this precept?

A. All unjust taking away, or detaining that which is another man's.

Q. 501. How many kinds of theft be there?

A. Three kinds, simple theft, which is a secret taking away that which is another man's; rapine, which is a taking away by open violence, or keeping of that which is another man's; and sacrilege, which is stealing of sacred things, or out of sacred places.

Q. 502. When is theft a mortal sin?

A. When the thing stolen is of a considerable value, or causeth a considerable hurt to our neighbour.

Q. 503. How prove you that:

A. Out of 1 Cor. vi. 10. "Neither thieves, nor covetous men, nor extortioners, shall possess the kingdom of God."

Q. 504. What doth the sin of theft oblige us to?

A. To make restitution of the things stolen to the right owner, if we be able, else the sin will not be forgiven us.

Q. 505. What else is here prohibited?

A. All usury, bribery, cozenage in gaming, or unjust gain by buying or selling.

Q. 506. What is usury?

A. It is to receive, or to hope for some money or moneys' worth, as gain, above the principle, immediately out of the consideration of loan.

Q. 507. How prove you usury and bribery to great sins?

A. Out of Psalm xiv. 1, 6. "O Lord, who shall dwell in thy tabernacle, or who shall rest in thy holy mountain? He that have not given his money to use, nor taken bribes upon the innocent man." And from Ezek. xxii 12. "Thou hast taken usury and increase, and hast covetously oppressed thy neighbours. I will disperse thee in the nations, and will scatter thee among the countries." Likewise from Luke vi. 35, where the Lord says, "Do good and lend, hoping for nothing thereby." See on this the Catechism of the holy council of Trent.

Q. 508. How are rich men soonest brought to beggary?

A. By mingling other men's goods among their own.

Q. 509. How do men generally sin against this precept?

A. Princes, by imposing unjust taxes on their subjects; subjects, by not paying their due taxes to their princes: buyers and sellers, by deceitful weight and measure, or by exceeding the just prices: masters by defrauding servants of their wages: and servants, by embezzling their master's goods. "And that no man over-reach or deceive his brother in business: because the Lord is the avenger of all such things, as we have told you before, and have testified." 1 Thess. iv. 6.

# The Eighth Commandment Expounded

Q. 510. What is the eighth commandment?

A. Thou shalt not bear false witness against thy neighbour.

Q. 511. What is prohibited by this precept?

A. All false testimonials, rash judgment, and lies.

Q. 512. Why is false testimony so great a sin?

A. Because it is against the justice of God, and our neighbour.

Q. 513. How prove you that corrupt judgment is a great sin?

A. Out of Isa. v. 22, 23, 24. "Wo be to you that call evil good, that justify the impious man for bribes and rob the just man of his justice; for as fire devoureth the stubble, so shall the root of these men be ashes."

Q. 514. Why is rash judgment a great sin?

A. Because it robs God of his judgment, and our neighbour of his good name: "Do not ye judge, that you be not judged." Matt. vii. 1.

Q. 515. Why is it a sin to lie?

A. Because "the devil is a liar, and the father of all lies." John viii. 44.

Q. 516. What else is prohibited by the precept?

A. The crimes of whispering, flattery, detraction.

Q. 517. What is whispering?

A. It is to break friendship between others, by speaking ill of one unto the other behind his back.

Q. 518. What is flattery?

A. to attribute to another some perfection which he hath not, or to praise him for that which he deserves not.

Q. 519. What is detraction?

A. Is is a secret staining and blotting another's good name.

Q. 520. What is calumny?

A. It is telling a falsehood of our neighbour to his prejudice.

Q. 521. Are lies, backbiting, flattery, afronts, detraction, and calumny, grievous sins?

A. They are often very grievous sins. The scriptures saith, Prov. vi. 16, 19. "Six things there are which the Lord hateth; and the seventh his soul destesteth. Haughty eyes, a lying tongue, hands that shed innocent blood, a heart that deviseth wicked plots, feet that are swift to run into mischief, a deceitful witness that uttereth lies, and him that soweth discord among the brethren.

Q. 522. What is he bound to, that hath hurt his neighbour in any of these kinds?

A. To make him satisfaction, and restore him his good name.

Q. 523. How for example?

A. If he have told a hurtful lie of him, he is bound to unsay it; or if he have revealed his secret sin, he is bound to speak well of the same party, and to mitigate the matter as well as he can.

Q. 524. Is it a sin to hearken to detraction?

A. To do it willingly, and with delight, or so as to encourage the detractor, it is; for by so doing we cooperate with the detractor.

Q. 525. How them must we behave ourselves among detractors?

A. If they be inferiors, we must reprehend them; if equals or superiors, we must show ourselves at least not pleased with that discourse.

Q. 526. What is rash judgment?

A. That which is grounded on mere hearsay, jealousy, and surmises without any moral certainty, or great probability.

Q. 527. When is a lie a mortal sin?

A. When it is any great dishonour to God or notable prejudice to our neighbour: otherwise, if it be merely officious, or trifling, it is but a venial sin.

# The Ninth and Tenth Commandments Expounded

Q. 528. What are the ninth and tenth commandments?

A. Thou shalt not covet thy neighbour's wife, Thou shalt not covet thy neighbour's goods.

Q. 529. What is prohibited by these commandments?

A. The inordinate will or desire of unlawful lust, especially adultery, and of all these.

Q. 530. What else?

A. Not only deliberate desire or consent, but likewise all voluntary delight and complacency, in covetous or impure thoughts and motions of the flesh.

Q. 531. How prove you that unchaste desires are mortal sins?

A. Out of Matt. v. 27, 28. "It was said of old, Thou shalt not commit adultery; but I say unto you, whosoever shall see a woman to lust after her, he hath already committed adultery in his heart."

Q. 532. How prove you covetous desires to be great sins?

A. Out of 1 Tim. vi. 9. "For they who would become rich, fall into temptation, and into the snare of the devil, and into many unprofitable and hurtful desires, which drown men in destruction and perdition."

Q. 533. Is there any sin in those motions of concupiscence, which we feel an suffer against our wills?

A. There is not, for nothing is sin, which is not voluntary and deliberate. Nay, if resisted they become the occasion of merit to us. To them were liable the most perfect saints, and even the apostles themselves; for Paul, 2 Cor. xii. 7, 8, 9, writes, "And lest the greatness of the revelations should puff me up, there was given me a sting of my flesh, and angel of Satan, to buffet me. For which thing I thrice besought the Lord, that it might depart from me: And he said to me: My grace is sufficient for thee: for power is made perfect in infirmity.

Q. 534. What think you now of this second table of the law, is there any thing that favours of impossibility?

A. No certainly, for there is nothing commanded us, which the very law of nature and right reason doth not dictate to us; and therefore ought to be observed and done, although it were not commanded us.

Q. 535. Is there any thing but What every man expects and desires to have done to himself by others?

A. There is not, therefore we must do the same to others, according to that, "All things Whatsoever you will that men do unto you, do ye also to them; for this is the law and the prophets." Matt. vii. 12.

Q. 536. Why then do Protestants pretend and say, that the commandments are impossible to be kept?

A. Because they are not willing to oblige themselves to the observance of them, but had rather make God the author of sin, by commanding impossibilities, (a most high blasphemy) and justify their own iniquities by saying, they cannot help it; than humbly acknowledge and confess their sins, with purpose to amend, by an acceptance of the law of God.

# The Precepts of the Church Expounded

Q. 537. How many are the commandments of the church?

A. There be six principle ones.

## The First Precept of the Church Expounded

Q. 538. What is the first?

A. "To hear mass on Sundays and holydays," if we have opportunity to do it, and there be no just cause to the contrary.

Q. 539. Why on all Sundays?

A. In thanksgiving for the benefits of the week past, as also to sanctify the Lord's day.

Q. 540. For What other reason?

A. In memory that the same Christ, who is offered upon the altar at the mass for our sins, was born, rose from the dead, and sent down the Holy Ghost on a Sunday.

Q. 541. Why on all holydays?

A. Either in memory of some special benefit, or else for a commemoration of some peculiar saint, so to move ourselves to imitate his example.

Q. 542. How prove you that the church hath power to ordain and command feasts?

A. First, by the example of the church in the apostle's time, which ordained the feast of Christmas in honour of the Nativity of Christ; Easter in honour of his resurrection; Whitsuntide, in honour of the coming of the Holy Ghost, in tongues of fire.

Secondly, out of St. Clement, the disciple of St. Peter, in his eighth book of apostolical constitutions, where he witnesseth. "That the apostles gave order for the celebrating of St. Stephen's and some other of their fellow apostles' days after their deaths."

Thirdly, out of 2 Thess. iii. 4. "And we have confidence concerning you in the Lord, that the things which we command, you both do, and will do." And ver. 14. "And if any man obey not our word by this epistle, note that man, and do not keep company with him, he may be ashamed."

Fourthly, out of 1 Thess. iv. 8, where St. Paul, (speaking of the precepts he had given his brethren,) saith, "He that despiseth these things, despiseth not man, but God, who also hath given his Holy Spirit in us." See What was said before in the third commandment of God.

## The Second Precept of the Church Expounded

Q. 543. What is the second commandment of the church?

A. To fast Lent, Vigils commanded, Ember days, and with abstinence from flesh on Fridays and Saturdays.

Q. 544. Why Lent?

A. In imitation of Christ our Lord, who fasted forty days and forty nights in the desert for our sins, without once eating or drinking.

Q. 545. Can we fast in this manner?

A. We cannot; but we must do at least What we are able.

Q. 546. How prove you fasting to be a pious practice?

A. By the example of Christ and his Saints, and out of Luke ii. 37, where we read, "That Anna the prophetess departed not from the temple serving day and night by fasting and prayer."

Q. 547. How prove you fasting to me meritorious?

A. Out of Matt. vi. 16, 17, 18. "And when you fast, be not sad, like the hypocrites; but anoint thy head, and wash thy face, that thou appear not unto men to fast, but to thy Father which is in secret, and thy Father who seeth in secret, will repay thee."

Q. 548. How prove you abstinence from certain meats to be commendable?

A. Because it was proscribed by an angel to St. John. "He shall be great before the Lord, wine and cider he shall not drink." Luke i. 15. And in Matt. iii. 4, we read, "That his food was locusts and wild honey."

Q. 549. For What is fasting available?

A. For the remission of sins and appeasing the wrath of God, according to that, "Be ye converted unto me in your whole heart, in fasting, weeping, and mourning," Joel ii. 12. To mortify all the lustful desires of the flesh; and that it hath special force against the Devil: "This kind of devil (saith our Lord) can go out by nothing but by prayer and fasting," Mark ix. 29.

Q. 550. Why Vigils?

A. To prepare ourselves for a devout keeping the feasts that follow.

Q. 551. Why Ember-days?

A. Because on those days the church giveth Holy orders and ordained priests; and for that cause hath dedicated them to public prayers and fasting.

Q. 552. What ground have you for that?

A. Out of Acts xiii. 2, 3. "And as they (the apostles) were ministering to our Lord, and fasting, the Holy

86

Ghost said, Separate ye unto me Saul and Barnabas to the work whereto I have them. Then with fasting and praying, and imposing hand on them, they dismissed them."

Q. 553. Why abstinence on Fridays?

A. In memory that Christ suffered for us upon a Friday; drinking gall and vinegar on the cross; but especially by custom, which is a good as law.

Q. 554. Why abstinence on Saturdays?

A. To prepare ourselves for a devout keeping of the Sunday, as also in honour of the blessed Virgin Mary, who stood firm in faith on that day, the apostles themselves wavering.

## The Third Precept of the Church Expounded

Q. 555. What is the third commandment of the church?

A. To confess our sins at least once a year.

Q. 556. Why was that commanded?

A. Because otherwise, libertines would not have done it once in many years.

## The Fourth Precept of the Church Expounded

Q. 557. What is the fourth?

A. To receive the blessed Sacrament at least once a year, and that at Easter, or thereabouts.

Q. 558. Why at Easter?

A. Because Christ instituted the blessed Sacrament of the Eucharist at his last supper, the Thursday before Easter day. Q. 559. What said it, or thereabouts?

A. Because it will satisfy the precept, if it be done at any time between Palm Sunday and Low-Sunday.

## The Fifth Precept of the Church Expounded

Q. 560. What is the fifth?

A. To pay tithes to our pastors.

Q. 561. Why so?

A. Because as they feed us spiritually, it is fit we should feed them corporally.

Q. 562. How prove you that?

A. Out of Gal. vi. 6. Let him that is catechised in the word communicate to him that catechised him, in all his goods. And 1 Cor. ix. 13, 14. They that serve the altar participate with the altar, and so the Lord ordained that they who preach the gospel should live by the gospel.

## The Sixth Precept of the Church Expounded

Q. 563. What is the sixth?

A. Not to solemnize marriage on times prohibited that is, from the first Sunday of Advent, until Twelfth day be past, nor from Ash-Wednesday, until Low-Sunday be past.

Q. 564. Why so?

A. Because those are times of special piety and penance, and should not therefore be spent in feasting, or carnal pleasures.

Q. 565. What sin is to break any of these church commandments?

A. A mortal sin of disobedience, according to that "He that will not hear the church, let him be unto thee as a heather and a publican." Matt. xvii. 17.

# The Counsel of Christ and his Church Expounded

Q. 566. How many counsels are there?
A. There be three principle ones.

## The First Counsel

Q. 567. What is the first of them?
A. Voluntary poverty, which is observed by willingly leaving all things to follow Christ.
Q. 568. How prove you that to be a work of perfection?
A. Out of Matt. xix. 21. "If thou wilt be perfect, go, sell What thou hast, and give to the poor, and thou shalt have treasure in heaven, and come and follow me."
Q. 569. How prove you this to be meritorious?
A. Out of the same chap. ver. 27, 28, 29, "When Peter, answering, said to him: Behold, we have left all things, and have followed he: What, therefore, shall we have? And Jesus said to them: Amen I say to you, that you, who have followed me, in the regeneration, when the Son of man shall sit on the seat of his majesty, you also shall sit on twelve seats judging the twelve tribes of Israel. And every one that hath left house, or brethren, or sisters, or father, or mother, or wife, or lands for my name's sake, shall receive a hundredfold and shall possess life everlasting."

## The Second Counsel

Q. 570. What is the second counsel?
A. Perpetual chastity; which is a voluntary abstaining from marriage, and all carnal pleasures, for the love of God.
Q. 571. Is this also a work of perfection?

A. It is, for Christ himself was born of a virgin, and counselled virginity, though he commanded it not.

Q. 572. How prove you that?

A. Out of Matt. xix. 12. "There be eunuchs, (said he,) which have made themselves so for the kingdom of heaven; he that can take let him take."

Q. 573. How prove you that virginity is a more prefect state than marriage, or that it is lawful to vow virginity?

A. Out of 1 Cor. vii. 37, 38. "He that hath determined in his heart, being settled, not having any necessity, but having power of his own will to keep his virgin, doth well; therefore he that joineth his virgin in marriage doth well, but he that joineth her not, doth better"

Q. 574. What other proof have you?

A. Out of 1 Tim. v. 5. "But she that is a widow indeed, (that is, a vowed widow,) and desolate, let her hope in God, and continue in prayer and supplications night and day." And ver. 11, 12. "But the younger widows avoid, for they, when they shall be wanton in Christ, will marry, having damnation, because they have made void their first faith, that is, their vow of chastity, according to the fourth council of Carthage, Canon 104, and all the Fathers."

Q. 575. Who was the first that taught marriage to be better than virginity, and persuaded priests and nuns to marry?

A. Jovinian, an old condemned Heretic, according to St. Augustin, in his book Heresies, Her. 82, and in his 2d book of Retractions, he calls him a monster for it, and saith the church stoutly resisted him, chap. 22.

## The Third Counsel

Q. 576. What is the third counsel?

A. Obedience, which is a voluntary submission to another's will, and in all that is not sin.

Q. 577. What warrant have you for that?

A. First the example of Christ himself, who was obedient to our Lady and St. Joseph, "And he went down with them and came to Nazareth, and was subject to them." Luke ii. 51.

Secondly, Heb. xiii. 17. "Obey your prelates, and be subject to them; for they watch, being to render an account for your souls."

# Of the Sacraments in general

Q. 578. How many Sacraments are there?

A. Seven.

Q. 579. How call you them?

A. Baptism, Confirmation, Eucharist, Penance, Extreme Unction, Holy Order, and Matrimony. See the Council of Trent, Sess. 7. Can. 1.

Q. 580. Is there any cause Why the number of Sacraments should be seven?

A. Yes; a probable cause is the proportion which is between spiritual and corporal life.

Q. 581. In What consists this proportion?

A. In this; that as in a corporal and nature life, there be seven principle or chief necessities, so are there likewise seven spiritual, to which the seven Sacraments correspond.

Q. 582. What is our first corporal necessity?

A. To be born into this world: to this baptism corresponds, by which we are regenerated unto God, and born the heirs of God and co-heirs of Christ.

Q. 583. What is the second corporal necessity?

A. To be confirmed in our strength and growth, without which we can never be made men: to this answers confirmation, by which we are made strong and perfect Christians, able to profess our faith before our enemies.

Q. 584. What is our third corporal necessity?

A. That (being now made men) we have a competence of daily food and sustenance; to which the blessed Eucharist corresponds, by which our souls are fed with divine grace as often as we worthily receive it, or offer it with the priest on the altar.

Q. 585. What is the fourth necessity of the body?

A. That we have physic when we are sick and wounded; to this the sacrament of penance answers; by which our maladies and sores of sin are healed.

Q. 586. What is our fifth necessity of the body?

A. That we have the necessary helps against the agonizing pangs of death; to this corresponds extreme unction, by which our soul is strengthened in her last agony, against the violent assaults of the devil.

Q. 587. What is the sixth corporal necessity?

A. "That we be governed by laws and magistrates, so to avoid injustice and confusion:" to this Holy Order corresponds, by which we are provided with spiritual magistrates to guide and govern us.

Q. 588. What is the seventh corporal necessity?

A. That we be multiplied in a lawful manner; and to this matrimony corresponds, by which we are not only multiplied in a natural, but in a holy and sacramental way.

Q. 589. What is a Sacramental in general?

A. It is a visible sign of invisible grace, divinely instituted by Christ, for our sanctification.

Q. 590. How prove you that Christ ordained them all?

A. Because it is not in the power of any pure creature to give infallible virtue, causing grace, to sensible and material things, such as the sacraments are; according to the council of Trent, Sess. 7. Can. 1.

Q. 591. From What have the Sacraments their force and efficacy?

A. From the blood and passion of Christ, which they apply to our souls.

Q. 592. How prove you that?

A. Rom. vi. 3. "Know you not that all that we who are baptized in Christ Jesus, are baptized in his death?" Rom. v. 9. "Much more therefore, now being justified in his blood, shall we be saved from wrath by him."

Q. 593. For What end did Christ ordain the Sacraments?

A. To be external and visible marks and professions of his holy faith, by which the faithful might be known from Infidels and Heretics; and also to be effectual means of our salvation, and certain remedies against sin.

Q. 594. What things are essential to a Sacrament?

A. Matter and form.

Q. 595. Do all the seven Sacraments give grace?

A. They do, according to the council of Trent, Sess. 7.

Q. 596. What is grace?

A. It is a supernatural quality produced in our souls and inherent in them, by which we are made the adopted children of God, special partakers of the divine nature, and like to God, in some degree; as iron is made like to fire by heat.

Q. 597. How many of these Sacraments give character?

A. Three: Baptism, Confirmation, and Holy Order.

Q. 598. What is a sacramental character?

A. It is a supernatural mark in the soul, whereby be are marked for God's servants, which can never be blotted out.

Q. 599. In What manner do the sacraments give and cause grace?

A. As a means or instruments only; for God is always the principal cause thereof.

Q. 600. Who is the ordinary minister of a Sacrament?

A. A priest; excepting Holy Orders and Confirmation, which are referred to the Bishops alone.

Q. 601. Why did Christ confine the administration of the Sacraments to the Heirarchy and to the priests only?

A. "O the depth of the riches, of the wisdom and of the knowledge of God! How incomprehensible are his judgments, and How unsearchable his ways! For who hath known the mind of the Lord? Or who hath been his counsellor?" Rom. xi. And we know from St. Paul, Ephes. iv. 11, that "Christ gave indeed some to be apostles, and some prophets, and others evangelists, and others pastors and teachers. That we may not now be children, tossed to and fro, and carried about with every wind of doctrine, in the wickedness of men, in craftiness by which they lie in wait to deceive." Hence, St. Paul, speaking of the Sacraments, says, 1 Cor. iv. 1. "So let them consider us as the ministers of Christ and dispensers of the mysteries of God." "And we are (2 Cor. v. 20.) therefore ambassadors of Christ: God, as it were, exhorting by us."

Q. 602. Is the intention of the ministers to do What Christ ordained, a condition, without which the Sacraments subsist not?

A. It is; also the intention of the receiver to receive What Christ ordained, if he be at the years of understanding?

Q. 603. Why say you, If he be at the years of understanding?

A. Because for infants in the Sacraments of baptism the intention of the Church sufficeth.

# Baptism Expounded

Q. 604. Why is Baptism the first Sacrament?

A. Because by it we are born again, or created anew in Christ Jesus, and therefore before it we are not capable of receiving any other.

Q. 605. What is Baptism?

94

A. It is an exterior washing of the body, under a set form of words.

Q. 606. What is the necessary matter of Baptism?

A. Natural water only; for artificial water will not suffice.

Q. 607. What is the form of it?

A. I baptize thee in the name of the Father, and of the Son, and of the Holy Ghost.

Q. 608. What if a man leave out the word, (I baptize) or any of the three persons?

A. Then the baptism is invalid.

Q. 609. Where did Christ express the form of baptism and give a command to baptize?

A. In Matt. xxvii. 29. "Go therefore, (saith he) teach ye all nations, baptizing them in the name of the Father, and of the Son, and of the Holy Ghost."

Q. 610. Can a man be saved without baptism?

A. He cannot, unless he have it either actual or in desire, with contrition, or to be baptized in his blood as the holy Innocents were, which suffered for Christ.

Q. 611. How prove you that?

A. Out of John iii. 5. "Unless a man be born again of water, and the Holy Spirit, he cannot enter into the kingdom of God."

Q. 612. Can no man but a priest baptize?

A. Yes, in case of necessity, any layman or woman may do it, and not otherwise.

Q. 613. What is a chief necessity?

A. When a child is in danger of death, and a priest cannot be had.

Q. 614. What are the effects of baptism?

A. It makes us the children of God, and remits both original and actual sin, if he that is baptized be guilty of it.

Secondly, it infuseth justifying grace into the soul, with habits of faith, hope, and charity, and all supernatural gifts and virtues.

Q. 615. How prove you that?

A. Out of Gal. iii. 27. "As many of you as are baptized in Christ, have put on Christ." Secondly, out of 1 Cor. vi. 10,11 where speaking of fornicators, idolators, thieves, adulterers, and liars "These things, (saith St. Paul) ye were, but ye are washed, but ye are sanctified, but ye are justified in the name of our Lord Jesus Christ, and in the spirit of God."

Thirdly, out of Tit. v. 6, 7. "He hath saved us by the laver of regeneration and renovation of the Holy Ghost, whom he hath abundantly poured out upon us, by Jesus Christ our Saviour, that being justified by his grace we may be heirs, according to the hope of life everlasting."

Q. 616. What other effect hath baptism?

A. It makes a spiritual mark or character in the soul, which shall remain for ever, either to our great joy in heaven, or our confusion in hell.

Q. 617. What sin is it to baptize a man twice?

A. A mortal sin of sacrilege.

Q. 618. How prove you that?

A. Out of Heb. vi. 4, 5, 6. "It is impossible for those that have been illuminated, and made partakers of the Holy Ghost, (to wit, by baptism) and are fallen, &c. to be renewed again unto penance," &c. viz. by a second baptism.

Q. 619. What if a man die for the faith, before he can be baptized?

A. He is a true martyr, and baptized in his own blood.

Q. 620. Why have we a Godfather and a Godmother in baptism?

A. That if our parents should neglect it, or be prevented by death, they may instruct us in the faith of Christ, which obligation lies on them.

Q. 621. How many godfathers may we have?

A. But one godfather and one godmother, since the council of Trent.

Q. 622. Why so few?

A. To prevent the too great spread of spiritual affinity, which is contracted between them and their godchild, and his father and mother, which is an impediment, that makes the marriage not only unlawful, but also invalid between the parties.

Q. 623. How can infants be christened, which have no actual faith?

A. In the faith of the Church, and of their godfathers and godmothers.

Q. 624. Who do we use so many ceremonies in baptism?

A. To stir up reverence to the sacrament, and signify its inward effects.

Q. 625. What meaneth the priest's breathing on the child's face, according to the use of some rituals?

A. It signifies, that by baptism, the evil spirit is cast out, and the spirit of God is given him.

Q. 626. Why is the child signed on the breast and forehead with the sign of the Cross?

A. To signify that he is there made the servant of Christ crucified.

Q. 627. Why is salt put into the child's mouth?

A. To signify, that by baptism he receives grace and gifts to preserve his soul from corruption of sin: and to warn Christians, that their actions and words ought to be seasoned with prudence and discretion signified by salt.

Q. 628. Why doth the priest lay spittle on his ears and nostrils?

A. Because Christ by so doing, healed one that was both deaf and dumb; as also to signify, that by baptism his ears are opened to the word of faith, and his nostrils to the good odour of all Christian virtues.

Q. 629. Why doth the priest ask the child, "If he renounce the Devil, and his pomps?"

A. To signify, that he who will be the child of God, cannot be the child of the Devil.

Q. 630. What means the several anointing of the child?

A. They signify the interior anointings, or unction of divine grace, given to the soul in baptism.

Q. 631. What mean they in particular?

A. He anointed on the head to signify, "that by baptism he is made partaker of the kingly dignity of Christ;" on the shoulders to signify, "he must bear his Cross courageously," on the breast, to signify, "that the heart is there strengthened with grace, to fight against the Devil."

Q. 632. What signifies the white garment given to the child?

A. The purity and innocence which he there receives.

Q. 633. What signifies the hallowed light given to the child?

A. The light of faith, and fire of charity with which his soul is endued by baptism; and that he is bound to hold up through life the lamp of good works, always burning, always shining before men, that they may glorify our Father who is in Heaven.

# Confirmation Expounded

Q. 634. What is the second Sacrament?

A. Confirmation.

Q. 635. When did Christ ordain this Sacrament?

A. The time is not certain; but divines most probably hold, it was instituted at Christ's last supper.

Q. 636. What is the matter of the Sacrament?

A. Oil, mingled with balm, blessed by a bishop.

Q. 637. What is the form of it?

A. I sign thee with the sign of the Cross, I confirm thee with the crism of salvation, in the name of the Father, and of the Son, and of the Holy Ghost.

Q. 638. What scripture have you for this Sacrament?

A. First, 2 Cor. i. 22. "And he that confirmeth us with you in Christ, and hath anointed us, is God, who also hath sealed us (with the spiritual character) and given the pledge of the spirit in our hearts.

Secondly, Acts viii. 14, 15, 16, where when Philip the deacon had converted the city of Samaria to the faith, the apostles who were at Jerusalem, sent to two bishops, St. Peter and St. John, to confirm them; "who when they were come (saith the text) prayed for them, that they might receive the Holy Ghost; for he was not yet come upon any of them, but they were only baptized in the name of our Lord Jesus; then did they impose their hands upon them, and they received the Holy Ghost."

Thirdly, Acts xix. 5,6, where we read that St. Paul baptized and confirmed about twelve of St. John's disciples: "Hearing these things, they were baptized in the name of our Lord Jesus; and when St. Paul had imposed hands on them, the Holy Ghost came upon them."

Q. 639. Why is oil used in this Sacrament?

A. To signify that the principal and proper effect of it, is the interior unction of the Holy Ghost, which makes us perfect Christians, and able to profess our faith before persecuting tyrants.

Q. 640. Why is balm used in it?

A. To signify the good odour of a Christian name, according to that, "We are a good odour of Christ to God." 2 Cor. ii. 15.

Q. 641. In What appears the effects of confirmation?

A. In the undaunted confidence and sufferings of the apostles, martyrs, and saints of God, after they had received it.

Q. 642. When were the apostles confirmed?

A. On Whitsunday, in an extraordinary manner, the Holy Ghost descended upon them in tongues of fire.

Q. 643. Doth confirmation give a character?

A. It doth, according to 2 Cor. i. 22, above cited, where we read "who also has sealed us," (that is, with a character.)

Q. 644. Who is the minister of this Sacrament?

A. A bishop only, as appears by Acts viii, above cited, where two bishops were sent into Samaria, to give it.

Q. 645. Is there any necessity for this Sacrament?

A. There is a moral necessity for it, according to the council of Laodicea, Can. 48:

"Those that have been baptized, must after baptism receive the most holy chrism, and be made partakers of the heavenly kingdom."

Q. 646. What authority of fathers and school divines have you for its necessity?

A. First, the authority of St. Thomas, who in the Sacrament of confirmation, 3P. Q.72, Art. 8, ad 4, affirms that it is a dangerous thing to die without it. Secondly, that of St. Jerome, in his epistles against the Luciferians. "Dost thou not know also (saith he) that this is the custom of the churches, that hands should be imposed on such as they have been baptized, and so the Holy Ghost be invoked? Dost thou require to know where it is written? In the acts of the apostles, and though there were no authority of scripture for it, yet the consent of the whole world in this behalf, would be equal to a precept; for many other things also which are observed in the churches by tradition, do usurp unto themselves the authority of a written law." You see he owns it to be commanded in the scripture; and tho it were not so, yet to be equal to a precept, and have the authority of a written law, because it is an apostolical tradition, that such as have been baptized, must also be confirmed.

Q. 647. What authority of Popes have you for it?

A. First, that of St. Clement, pope and martyr, in his epistle to Julius, "All must make haste, (mark the word must) without delay to be regenerated to God, and at length consigned (confirmed) by a bishop; that is, to receive the same seven-fold grace of the Holy Ghost." His reason is, first, "Because the end of every one's life is uncertain," secondly, "Because otherwise he that is baptized, cannot be a perfect Christian, nor have a seat among the perfect; if not by necessity, he shall remain and not have that confirmation, which we have received from blessed Peter, and all the rest of the apostles have taught, or Lord commanding," Secondly, that of Pope Melchiades, teaching "That baptism and confirmation can by no means be separated one from another, unless by death prevented, and that one of them cannot rightly be perfected without the other. And moreover, that as confirmation is given by greater men, so it is to be held in greater veneration than baptism," see De Cons., Dist 5, Cap. De his. Add to this, that without confirmation (according to all the fathers) we are not perfect Christians.

Q. 648. What then would you think of those, who for particular and private ends, should slight this Sacrament, and teach the laity not to receive it, when they might conveniently have it?

A. Truly I think they would slight the mission of the Holy Ghost, (for this Sacrament is a continuance of that mission unto us) and would be great enemies of Christianity.

Q. 649. What sin is it not to receive it, when we may conveniently have it?

A. Mortal sin, if it be done out of contempt, or any gross neglect, especially in a place of persecution.

Q. 650. How prove you that?

A. Because by so doing we expose ourselves to great danger of denying the faith, against which danger, it was peculiarly ordained by Christ our Lord.

Q. 651. At What age is confirmation now commonly received?

A. At seven years old.

Q. 652. Why not sooner?

101

A. That so we may be able to prepare ourselves for it, and remember What we have received it; for it can not be twice given.

Q. 653. Why is a little blow given on the cheek to him that is confirmed?

A. To signify he is there made the soldier of Christ, and must be ready to suffer stripes and buffets for his sake.

Q. 654. Must we have any godfathers in confirmation?

A. Only one godfather or godmother.

Q. 655. Must it be received fasting?

A. That is expedient, (for so the apostles received) but not necessary.

## The Eucharist Expounded

Q. 656. What is the third Sacrament?

A. The blessed Eucharist, or the Sacrament of the body and blood of Christ.

Q. 657. By What was this Sacrament prefigured in the old law?

A. By the tree of life, the burning bush, Mechisedech's bread and wine, the Paschal Lamb, and the heavenly manna.

Q. 658. Doth the blessed Eucharist excel all these in dignity?

A. It doth, as far as the substantial body excels a shadow.

Q. 659. What signifies the name Eucharist?

A. It signifies good grace, or thanksgiving, because it contains the author and fountain of grace, and the greatest gift of God to man.

Q. 660. When did Christ ordain the blessed Eucharist?

A. At his last supper.

Q. 661. Why so?

A. To leave to his church, as the last and greatest pledge of his love.

Q. 662. What is the blessed Eucharist?

A. It is the body and blood of Jesus Christ, true God, and true man, under the outward forms of bread and wine.

Q. 663. In What manner is Christ present under these forms?

A. By the true and real presence of his divine and human nature.

Q. 664. How prove you that?

A. First out of Matt. xxvi. 27, 28. Christ at his last supper, took bread and blessed it, brake it and gave it to his disciples, saying, "Take eat, this is my body. And he blessed the cup saying, This is my blood of the New Testament which shall be shed for many to the remission of sins," Mark xiv. 22, 24.

Secondly, out of Luke xxii. 19, 20. "This is my body which is given for you, this is the chalice of the New Testament in my blood, which shall be shed for you."

Thirdly, out of John vi. 52, 53, 54. "The bread which I give is my flesh, for the life of the world; by flesh is meat indeed, and my blood is drink indeed; unless you eat the flesh of the Son of man, and drink his blood, you shall have no life in you."

Fourthly, out of 1 Cor. xi. 23, where St. Paul tells us, "He received from our Lord," (viz. by special revelation) that at his last supper he blessed bread, saying, "Take ye and eat, this is my body which shall be delivered up for you; this chalice is the New Testament in my blood."

Q. 665. By What means is the body and blood of Christ made under the outward forms of bread and wine?

A. By the real conversion or change of the whole substance of the body and blood of Christ; which conversion is wrought by the most holy and powerful words of consecration, instituted by Christ, and spoken by the priest, and is fitly called Transubstantiation, by the councils of Lateran and Trent; which signifies a passage or conversion of one substance into another.

Q. 666. Is there any scripture for Transubstantiation?

A. The word Transubstantiation is not found in scripture, but for the thing signified by it, there are those places in scripture, which prove a real presence, because those words, This is my Body, spoken by Christ, after he had taken bread into his hands, and signifying that to be his body, which before was bread, cannot be true, without the change of of bread into his body; which change is (as I have said already) the thing signified or meant by Transubstantiation. Nor may the word be lawfully rejected for not being found in scripture more than other words used by the church, to explain mysteries of faith; as the word, Trinity or Consubstantiality of God the Son with God the Father, which are not found in scripture.

Q. 667. What mean you by these species or accidents which remain after the substance of the bread is changed?

A. The colour, taste, and quality of bread.

Q. 668. Is the body of Christ divided or broken, when we divide or break the Sacrament?

A. It is not, for "he is now immortal and impassible, he cannot die nor suffer any more." Rom.vi. 9.

Q. 669. What other reason have you?

A. Because Christ is whole in the whole host, and whole in every particle thereof, if you divide or break it; seeing that wherever there would have been bread before consecration, there must needs be the whole body and blood of Christ after consecration.

Q. 670. What example have you for that?

A. The Soul of Man, which is whole in the whole body, and whole in every part of the body, as learned Protestants neither do nor can deny.

Q. 671. How can the same thing be in many several places at once?

A. By the omnipotent power of God, by which he himself is in all, and every one of his creatures at the same instant.

Q. 672. What example have you for that?

A. A word, which being one, yet is in many hundreds of places at once. Out of Acts ix. 4, 5, where we read, that Christ, who is always sitting at the right hand of the Father in Heaven (as we willingly admit with the Protestants) appeared notwithstanding, and discoursed with St. Paul on earth, saying, "Saul, Saul, Why dost thou persecute me?" And when St. Paul replied, "Who art thou, Lord? He answered, I am Jesus whom thou dost persecute." Therefore, he was then in two places at once.

Q. 673. What is the necessary matter of the Eucharist?

A. Wheaten bread and wine of the grape.

Q. 674. What is the essential form of it?

A. THIS IS MY BODY, THIS IS MY BLOOD.

Q. 675. Why is a little water mingled with the wine in the chalice?

A. To signify the blood and water flowing from the side of Christ; as also, the union of the faithful with Christ, by virtue of the Sacrament.

Q. 676. What dispositions is required in him that receives the Eucharist?

A. That he hath first confessed his sins, and be in the state of grace.

Q. 677. How prove you that?

A. Out of 1 Cor. xi. 28. "Let a man prove himself and so let him eat of this bread and drink of this cup. For he that eateth and drinketh unworthily, eateth an drinketh damnation to himself, not discerning the body of our Lord."

Q. 678. What are the effects of the Eucharist?

A. It replenisheth the soul with grace, and nourisheth it in spiritual life: "He that eateth of this bread, shall live for ever," John vi. 58.

Q. 679. What other benefit have we by it?

A. It is a most moving and effectual commemoration of the incarnation, nativity, passion, resurrection, and ascension of Christ.

Q. 680. How do you prove it lawful for the laity, to communicate under one kind only?

A. First, because there is no command in scripture for the laity to do it under both, though there be for priests in those words, "Drink ye all of this." Matt. xxvi. 27, which was spoken to the apostles only and by them fulfilled; for it follows in Mark xiv. 23. "And they all drank." 2. Out of John vi. 58, "He that eateth of this bread, shall live for ever," therefore, one kind sufficeth. 3. Out of Acts xx. 7, where we read, "That the faithful were assembled on the first of the sabbath to break bread," without any mention of the cup; and the two disciples in Emmaus, "knew Christ in the breaking of bread," where the cup is not mentioned. And St. Paul, 1 Cor. xi. 27. "Wherefore whosoever shall eat this bread, or drink the chalice of the Lord unworthily shall be guilty of the body and blood of the Lord."

Q. 681. What is the exterior visible sacrifice?

A. It a most necessary act of religion whereby some sensible thing is offered to God by a priest, in order to acknowledge his supreme dominion over us, and our entire dependence on him. It is offered to God as an act of pure adoration, or to render him thanks for his benefits received, or to turn away his anger, or to obtain from him some new blessing, or for all those purposes together.

Q. 682. Is the blessed Eucharist a sacrifice?

A. It is a clean oblation, which the prophet Malachy i. 11, foretold would be offered from the rising to the going down of the sun, in every place among the Gentiles; which was prefigured by Melchisedech, priest of the Most High (Gen. xiv. 18,) when he brought forth bread and wine; and which was, in reality, instituted at the last supper by Jesus Christ, when he took bread and wine, blessed them, and distributed them with his own hands amongst the apostles, saying, THIS IS MY BODY; THIS IS MY BLOOD. Christ Jesus is a priest for ever, according to the order of Melchisedech (Heb. v. 8,) and so he instituted, according to his order; that is to say, in bread and wine, this great sacrifice of the NEW LAW.

All the Holy Popes, and Fathers, and Councils of the primitive ages, teach that the mass is the self same sacrifice of bread and wine that had been instituted by our Saviour; whilst the histories and annals of all countries, not excepting England herself, declare that the Holy Mass, but no other sacrifice, came down to them as a part and parcel of Christianity, from the apostolic age.

Q. 683. Why are the priests obliged to receive under both kinds?

A. Because they offer sacrifice, and represent the bloody sacrifice made upon the cross, where the blood was actually divided from the body, and being offerers of the sacrifice, are bound to receive also the cup, by Christ's command expressed. Matt. xxvi. 27. "Drink ye all of this."

Q. 684. Did the laity ever communicate under both kinds?

A. They did sometimes in the primitive church, and may again, if holy church shall so appoint; but now it is prohibited by the church, to prevent the great danger of shedding the cup, neither are the laity in this defrauded of any thing; for they receive whole Christ under one kind, which is incomparably more than the pretended reformers have under both, who receive only a bit of baker's bread, with a cup of common vintner's wine. See "Holy Order expounded." See also, "The Mass expounded." ch. 22.

# Penance Expounded

Q. 685. What is the fourth Sacrament?

A. Penance.

Q. 686. What warrant have you for doing acts of penance?

A. First, out of Apoc. ii. 4. "Thou hast left thy first charity, therefore be mindful from whence thou art fallen, and do penance?"

Secondly, "And JESUS began to preach, and say, do ye penance; for the kingdom of heaven is at hand." Matt. iv. 17.

Q. 687. When did Christ ordain this Sacrament?

A. When he breathed on his disciples, saying, "Receive ye the Holy Ghost, whose sins ye shall forgive, they are forgiven and whose sins ye shall retain, they are retained." John xx. 22, 23.

Q. 688. What is the matter of this Sacrament?

A. The sins and confession of the penitent.

Q. 689. What is the form of it?

A. I absolve thee from they sins, in the name of the Father, and of the Son, and of the Holy Ghost.

Q. 690. What are the effects of it?

A. It reconciles us to God, and either restores or increases grace?

Q. 691. How prove you that?

A. Out of John xx. 23, before cited. And out of John i. 9. "If we confess our sins, he is faithful and just to forgive us our sins, and cleanse us from all iniquity."

Q. 692. How many parts hath the Sacrament of penance?

A. It hath three parts; namely, contrition, confession, and satisfaction.

Q. 693. What is contrition?

A. It is a hearty sorrow for our sins, proceeding immediately from the love of God above all things, and joined with a firm purpose of amendment.

Q. 694. What is attrition?

A. It is imperfect contrition, arising from the consideration of the turpitude of sin, or fear of punishment and if it contain a detestation of sin, and hope of pardon, it is so far from being itself wicked, that though alone it justify not, yet it prepares the way to justification; and disposes it at least remotely towards obtaining God's grace in this Sacrament.

Q. 695. What if a dying man be in mortal sin, and cannot have a priest.

A. Then nothing but perfect contrition will suffice, it being impossible to be saved, without the love of God.

Q. 696. What is a firm purpose of amendment?

A. It is a resolution not only to shun sin, but also the occasions of it.

Q. 697. How long has confession been in use and practice?

A. Ever since the Apostle's time, according to James, v. 16. "Confess therefore your sins to one another, and pray for one another, that you may be saved." And Acts xix. 18. "Many of them that believed came confessing and declaring their deeds."

Q. 698. What is confession?

A. It is a full, sincere, and humble declaration of our sins to a priest, to obtain absolution.

Q. 699. Is there any special good or comfort to man from confession?

A. Very great, because as to a mind laden with secret griefs, the best of comforts is to disclose her case to some faithful friend; so to a soul laded with secret sins one of the greatest comforts, and best remedies possible, is to have selected persons ordained for that end by Christ himself, men of singular piety and learning, and not questionable by any law of What they hear in confession, to whom one may confess his sins, with an assurance both of comfort, correction, and direction for the amendment of his faults.

Q. 700. What are the necessary conditions of a good confession?

A. That it be short, diligent, humble, sorrowful, sincere, and entire.

Q. 701. How, short?

A. By avoiding superfluous words and circumlocutions.

Q. 702. How, diligent?

A. By using a competent time and care in the examining of our conscience.

Q. 703. How, humble?

A. By making our confession with humble hearts.

Q. 704. How, sorrowful?

A. By stirring up sorrow for our sins.

Q. 705. How, sincere?

A. By confessing our sins plainly, without seeking to lessen or excuse them.

Q. 706. How, entire?

A. By confessing not only in What things we have sinned mortally, but also How often, as near as we are able to remember.

Q. 707. What if a man do knowingly leave out any mortal sin in his confession for fear of shame?

A. He makes his whole confession void, and commits a great sacrilege by lying to the Holy Ghost, and abusing the Sacrament.

Q. 708. How prove you that?

A. By the example of Ananias and his wife Saphna, who were struck dead at the feet of St. Peter, for daring to lie to the Holy Ghost. Acts v. 5, 10.

Q. 709. Is he that hath so done bound to confess all again?

A. Yes, all that are mortal, together with that which he left out, and the sacrilege he committed.

Q. 710. What is satisfaction?

A. The sacramental penance, enjoined us by the priest at confession, (which is considered a part of this sacrament,) besides which we may also add more, for our own sins, by our voluntary prayers, fasting, or other good works, or sufferings.

Q. 711. For What do we satisfy by that penance?

A. For such temporal punishments as remain due sometimes for our sins, after they are forgiven us.

Q. 712. How do you prove that priests have power to impose penance?

A. Out of 1 Cor. vi. 3, where St. Paul excommunicated the incestuous Corinthian; "I (saith he) absent in body, but present in spirit, have already judged him that hath so done, &c. to deliver such a one to Satan for the destruction of the flesh, that the soul may be saved." ver. 5.

Q. 713. How prove you that temporal punishments may remain due for our sins, after the sins themselves be forgiven us?

A. First, because Adam, after his sin was forgiven him, was notwithstanding cast out of paradise for ever, and his whole posterity made subject unto death and many miseries, in punishment of that sin. Gen. iii. 25.

Secondly, because David, after his sin of adultery was forgiven him, was temporally punished for it with the death of his child: "Our Lord (saith Nathan) hath taken away thy sin, nevertheless thy son shall die." 2 Kings xii. 13, 14.

Thirdly, because "Whom our Lord loveth he chastiseth." Heb. xii. 6.

Q. 714. By What other means are those temporal punishments released?

A. By indulgences.

Q. 715. What is an indulgence?

A. No a pardon for sins to come, or leave to commit sin, (as Protestants do falsely and slanderously teach) but a releasing only of such temporal punishments, as remain due to those sins, which have already been forgiven us by penance and confession.

Q. 716. How doth an indulgence release those punishments?

A. By the superabundant merits of Christ and his saints, which it applies to our souls by the special grant of the church.

Q. 717. When did Christ give his church power to grant indulgences?

A. When he said to St. Peter, "To thee will I give the keys of the kingdom of Heaven, Whatsoever thou shalt bind on earth, it shall be bound in Heaven, and Whatsoever thou shalt loose on earth, shall be loosed in Heaven." Matt. xvi. 19.

Q. 718. How prove you that the apostles did ever use this power?

A. Out of 2 Cor. ii. 10, where St. Paul remitted part of the Corinthians penance. "To him that is such a one (said he) this rebuke sufficeth, &c. whom you have pardoned any thing, I also pardon."

Q. 719. What is required for the gaining an indulgence"

A. That we perform the works enjoined us, and that the last part of them be done in a state of grace.

Q. 720. What are those works?

A. Fasting, prayer, and alms deeds; as also confession and communion.

## Extreme Unction Expounded

Q. 721. What is the fifth Sacrament?

A. Extreme unction. [1]

---

[1]   Unction is twofold, exterior and interior; by the former is the body anointed, and the latter the soul: there is an instance of the former in James v. 14, and of the latter in the parable of the ten virgins, Matt. xxv. The exterior anointing of the body is expressive of the interior unction or invisible grace produced in the soul. Under the Old Law were the priests, prophets and kings anointed: 1 Kings

Q. 722. When did Christ institute it?

A. The time is uncertain: some think it was instituted at his last supper; others that it was done between his resurrection and ascension.

Q. 723. By whom was this sacrament promulgated?

A. By James, v. 13, 14, 15. "Is any man sick among you, let him bring in the priests of the church, and let them pray over him, anointing him with oil, in the name of our Lord, and the prayer of faith shall save the sick man, and our Lord will lift him up, and if he be in sin his sins shall be forgiven him."

Q. 724. Who is capable of this sacrament?

A. Every true and faithful Christian who is in mortal danger of death by sickness, excepting infants, fools, and such as are always mad.

Q. 725. What is the matter of it?

A. Oil blessed by a bishop.

Q. 726. What is the form of it?

A. "By his own anointing, and his own most pious mercy, our Lord pardon thee, Whatsoever thou hast sinned by thy seeing," &c. And so of the other senses, repeating the same words.

Q. 727. What are the effects of extreme unction?

---

ix. 16; 2 Kings ii. 4; and 3 Kings xix. 15.Our Blessed Redeemer is called the Anointed, from the Greek verb Krio which signifies to anoint, because God anointed hem with the Holy Ghost: Acts x. 38. And we are called Christians because we profess the law and doctrine of God, the Anointed; and because we are anointed with holy oil and chrism. The child is anointed at baptism, the priest in receiving Holy Orders, the king and queen at their coronation. That the Apostles anointed the sick is clear from Mark vi. 13, and that they taught the practice is clear from James v. 14. Would they teach or practise the rite if they had not commission from their Divine Master so to do? It is indeed extremely astonishing that the Protestants who pretend to be enamoured with the Bible would discard a rite so sanctioned in both Testaments and the usage of all antiquity. See Canons. Lib. i. Cit. 15.

A. It comforts the soul in her last agony against despair, it remits venial sins and removes the relics of sin and restores corporal health, if it be expedient.

Q. 728. How prove you that?

A. Out of Mark vi. 13, where we read, That the apostles anointed with oil many sick, and healed them. Which anointing is understood by many to have been a previous sign of extreme unction, and consequently of its effects.

Q. 729. Why then do so few recover after it?

A. Either because the recovery of the body is not expedient for the soul, or because the sick deferred the sacrament too long, as too many do, or for the other indispositions in the receiver of it

# Holy Order Expounded

Q. 730. What is the sixth Sacrament?

A. Holy Order.

Q. 731. To whom doth this appertain?

A. To the rulers and ministers of the church, as bishops, priests, deacons, and subdeacons.

Q. 732. What proof have you for bishops, priests and deacons?

A. For bishops and deacons, out of Phil. i. 1. "To all the saints at Philippi, (saith St. Paul)

with the bishops and deacons," and for the priests out of St. James above cited. "Is any man sick among you, let him bring in the priests of the church." &c.

Q. 733. Where did Christ ordain this Sacrament?

A. At his last supper, where he made his Apostles priests, saying, "This is my body which is given for you; do ye this in commemoration of me." Luke xxii. 19.

Q. 734. What did Christ give them power to do?

A. To offer the unbloody sacrifice of his own body and blood, which he himself had there ordained, and offered under the outward forms of bread and wine.

Q. 735. Why did he say, Do ye this in commemoration of me?

A. Because the unbloody sacrifice of the Mass is a commemoration or memorial of the unbloody sacrifice made on the Cross; nay more, it is a renewal of it in an unbloody manner.

Q. 736. What are the effects of holy order?

A. It gives spiritual power, to ordain priests, to consecrate the body and blood of Christ, to administer the sacraments, serve the altar, and to preach.

Q. 737. What else?

A. It gives also a spiritual grace, for the well-doing of these offices.

Q. 738. How prove you that?

A. Out of 1 Tim. iv. 14. "Neglect not the grace which is thine by prophecy, with the imposition of the hands of the priesthood."

Q. 739. What is the proper office of a bishop?

A. To give holy orders and confirmation, to preach and govern the church.

Q. 740. How prove you that?

A. To confirm, out of Acts viii. above cited, where we read, "Two bishops were sent to confirm the Samaritans."

Q. 741. How prove you that the bishops are of divine right and have authority from God to rule the church?

A. Out of Acts xx. 28. "Take heed unto yourselves and to the whole flock, wherein the Holy Ghost hath made you bishops to rule the church of God."

Q. 742. How prove you that the bishops only can ordain priests?

A. Out of Titus i. 5. "For this cause left I thee in Crete, that thou shouldest order the things that were wanting, and ordain priests in every city," (he was a bishop.)

Q. 743. What sin is it therefore to oppose Hierarchy and Episcopacy either in the whole church, or in particular churches?

A. It is a sin of rebellion and high treason against the peace and safety of Christ's spiritual commonwealth, the church.

Q. 744. How prove you that?

A. Because no law can subsist without guards and officers for it. Since therefore Christ hath ordained bishops to be the guards and teachers of his law, they who strike at bishops, strike also at the whole law of Christ, and safety of the people.

Q. 745. Why is it requisite that bishops and pastors should have revenues?

A. Because they bear a considerable charge and office in the commonwealth, therefore, they ought to have a competence for the performance of it. Secondly, to enable them, as good soldiers of Christ Jesus, to keep clear of worldly cares: for "no man, being a soldier to God, entangleth himself with worldly business; that he may please him to whom he hath engaged himself." 2 Tim. ii. 4.

Q. 746. What is the office of a priest?

A. To offer sacrifice, and administer the rest of the sacraments, excepting holy order and confirmation.

Q. 747. How prove you a sacrifice in the New Law?

A. First, because there is a priesthood, as you have heard, and an altar according to that, "We have an altar (saith St. Paul) whereof they have not power to eat, who serve in the tabernacle." Heb. xiii. 10.

Secondly, out of Mal. i. 11, where he foretold the sacrifice in the new law, saying, "From the rising of the sun, even to the going down, great is my name among the Gentiles, and in every place there is sacrificing, and there is offered to my name a clean oblation, saith the Lord of Hosts."

Thirdly, out of Luke xxii. 19, 20, where Christ who is high priest for ever (according to the order of

Melchesedech) offered the sacrifice of his own body and blood under the form of bread and wine, saying, "This is my body which is given for you, (it is given for us, you find at his last supper) this is the chalice of the New Testament in my blood, which chalice (according to the great text) is shed for you."

Q. 748. Is it lawful for priests to marry?

A. It is not; there being a precept of the church against it, descending to us by tradition from the Apostles; neither did any of the Apostles ever accompany their wives, after their calling to the apostleship; and a vow of perpetual chastity being annexed to the holy orders, in the Latin or Western church.

Q. 749. Why is it requisite that priests should live chaste and unmarried?

A. Because, as by their ordination they are bound to teach and instruct the faithful, their minds should be totally disengaged from the cares and pleasures of the world, and wholly employed in the study and piety of heavenly things, which is incompatible with the marriage state. 1 Cor. vii. 32.

Q. 750. What are the lesser orders of the church?

A. Acolyte, lector, exorcist, and porter, according to the fourth council of Carthage, can. 6.

Q. 751. Is it lawful for women to preach, or to be priests?

A. It is not, according to 1 Cor. xiv. 34. "Let women keep silence in the churches: for it is not permitted to them to speak, but to the subject, as also the law saith."

Q. 752. It is lawful for a man to usurp and take upon him priestly power, without the ordination of the church?

A. It is not, according to Heb. v. 1, 4. "For every high priest taken from among men, is appointed for men &c. that he may offer gifts and sacrifices for sins neither doth any man take the honour to himself, but he that is called of God, as was Aaron.

Q. 753. What other proof have you?

A. Out of John x. 1. "Amen I say unto you, he that entereth not by the door (Holy Order) into the fold of the sheep, but climbs up another way, is a thief and a robber."

Q. 754. What if any man pretend an extraordinary calling?

A. He must prove it by miracles, or else be esteemed an impostor.

Q. 755. What examples have you against the usurpation of the priestly power?

A. That the king Ozeas, who was presently struck by God with a leprosy in his forehead, for usurping the priestly office of offering or burning incense in the temple. 2 Paral. Xxvi. 19.

Q. 756. What besides?

A. The example of Core, Dathan, and Abriam, who for usurping the office of priest, (though they were themselves true believers) were swallowed up alive by the earth, Numb. xvi. 32. and two hundred and fifty others who were offering incense with them, were consumed with fire from heaven, v. 34, with fourteen thousand and seven hundred more, which were also burnt with fire from heaven, for only joining with them, v. 49. Matrimony Expounded

Q. 757. What is the seventh Sacrament?

A. Matrimony.

Q. 758. Where was matrimony first ordained?

A. In paradise by Almighty God, when he gave Eve as wife to Adam, who presently said,

"Therefore a man shall leaven his father and his mother, and shall cleave unto his wife, and they shall be two in one flesh." Gen. ii. 22, 24.

Q. 759. Where was it made a sacrament of the new law?

A. Where and when Christ instituted this sacrament us uncertain; some think it done, or at least insinuated at the wedding at Cana in Galilee, where Christ was present, and wrought his first miracle, "by turning water into wine." John ii. Others, more probably, say it was done, when Christ declared the indissolubility of marriage, saying, "therefore now they are not two, but one flesh: that therefore which God hath joined together, let no man separate." Matt. xix. 6.

Q. 760. Why was it requisite that marriage should be made a sacrament?

A. Because it is a contract whereon depends the chief happiness of a married life; as being ordained for the restraint of sinful concupiscence, the good of posterity, the wellorderingour domestic affairs, and the education of our children in the fear and service of God, and therefore ought to be ranked in the highest order of those actions, which Christ hath sanctioned for the use of man.

Q. 761. What other proof have you?

A. Out of Ephes. v. 31, 32. "They shall be two in one flesh; this is the great sacrament. But I speak in Christ, and in the church."

Q. 762. What is the matter of this sacrament?

A. The mutual consent of the parties, and giving themselves to one another.

Q. 763. What are the effects of matrimony?

A. It gives special grace to the married couple, to love and bear on with another, as also to bring up their children in the fear and love of God.

Q. 764. What is the principle end of marriage?

A. To beget children, and bring them up in the service of God; and the next to this is, that man may have a remedy against concupiscence, and a helper in the way of salvation.

Q. 765. How great is the tie of marriage?

A. So great that it can never be dissolved but by death, as you have heard out of Matt. xix.

Q. 766. What are the obligations of man and wife?

A. To love, honour, and comfort one another.

Q. 767. What besides?

A. Husbands are obliged to cherish and comfort their wives; wives to be subject, obey, and love their husbands.

Q. 768. How prove you that?

A. Out of Col. iii. 18, 19. "Women be subject to your own husbands, as behooveth in our Lord. Men, love your wives, and be not bitter towards them." And out of Ephes. iv. 22, 23. "Let women be subject to their husbands, as to the Lord, because the man is head of the woman as Christ is head of the church," v. 24. "But as the Church is subject to Christ, so also women to their husbands in all things." And again, v. 33. "Let each man love his wife as himself, and let the wife reverence her husband.

Q. 769. What else?

A. To render mutually the marriage debt, and according to that, "Let the husband render his debt unto his wife, and the wife also in like manner to her husband. The women now hath no power of her own body, but the husband, and in like manner the man hath no power of his own body, but the woman." 1 Cor. vii. 3, 4.

Q. 770. It is lawful for children to marry without the consent of their parents?

A. It is not; neither is it lawful for parents to force them to marry against their will.

Q. 771. Why are so many unhappy in their marriages?

A. Because they never consulted with God about them, nor sought to have his blessing in them.

Q. 772. For What other reason?

A. Because they were in the state of sin at their marriage, or married for inordinate love or wealth, and not for the right end of marriage.

Q. 773. What meaneth the blessing of the priest given in marriage?

A. It is to beg all blessings of God for the new married couple.

Q. 774. Why is the ring put on the fourth finger?

A. Because that is called the heart finger and hath (they say) a vein in it, with reacheth to the heart; so to signify the true and constant love which ought to be between man and wife.

Q. 775. What signifies the ring itself?

A. It is a symbol of perfection and eternity, being equal in all parts, and round in figure, without beginning or end, to imitate the perfect and perpetual love of man and wife.

Q. 776. What are the spiritual means to obtain the blessing of good children?

A. Fasting, prayer, and alms-deeds, for so St. Joachim and St. Anne obtained Blessed Virgin Mary; and so the Blessed Virgin became the mother of God.

Q. 777. What obligations have parents to their children?

A. To instruct them in the faith of Christ, to bring them up in the fear of God, to give them good example, to keep them out of ill company and other occasions of sin, to feed and nourish them, to provide for them in marriage, and to correct their faults.

Q. 778. What are the chief and most common impediments of marriage?

A. Consanguinity and affinity, to the fourth degree inclusively; and in the right line all degrees are prohibited by the law of nature, indispensable.

Q. 779. Can the church dispense in these collateral degrees?

A. She can, excepting only the first collateral degrees of consanguinity, but always sufficient motives must be given.

Q. 780. How prove you that?

A. The Church having made these laws, for just reasons may dispense in them; but when such dispensations are given, those who seek them ought to consider, that they may deprive themselves of the blessings attending the marriage state, if the motives alleged be not well founded.

## The Cardinal Virtues Expounded

Q. 781. How many cardinal virtues are there?

A. There are four: prudence, justice, fortitude, and temperance.

Q. 782. Why are they called cardinal virtues?

A. Because they are the fountains and as it were the hinges of all good works, from the word Cardo, which signifies a hinge.

Q. 783. What is prudence?

A. It is a virtue which makes us wary in all our actions, that we may neither deceive others, nor be deceived ourselves; or which (according to the rule of honesty) prescribes us What to be desired, and What to be avoided.

Q. 784. How prove you that?

A. Out of Eccles. iii. 32. "A wise heart that hath understanding, will keep itself from all sin, and in the works of justice shall have success."

Q. 785. What is justice?

A. It is a virtue which gives every man this own according to that, "Render to all men their due, to whom tribute, tribute; to whom custom, custom; to whom fear, fear; to whom honour, honour." Rom. xiii. 7.

Q. 786. What is temperance?

A. It is a virtue which moderates our appetites and desires, that they be according to reason, and not inordinate: "He that is abstinate, (saith the wise man) shall increase in life." Eccl. xxxvii.

Q. 787. What is fortitude?

A. It is a virtue, by which the labours and dangers even of death itself, that are opposite unto virtue, are courageously undertaken and patiently sustained, "The wicked fleeth (saith Soloman) when no man pursueth; but the just man, as a confident lion, shall be without fear." Prov. xxvii. 1. And in 1 Pet. iii. 14, we read, "The fear of them fear ye not, and be not troubled, but sanctify our Lord Christ in your hearts."

Q. 788. Is it necessary for a Christian to be exercised in these virtues?

A. It is; for "we must not only decline from evil, but do good," Psalm xxxvi. 27.

# The Gifts of the Holy Ghost Expounded

Q. 789. How many are the Gifts of the Holy Ghost?

A. Seven: wisdom, understanding, counsel, fortitude, knowledge, piety, and the fear of the Lord. Isa. xi. 2.

Q. 790. What is wisdom?

A. It is a gift of God, which teacheth us to direct our whole lives and actions to his honour, and the salvation of our souls.

Q. 791. What is understanding?

A. It is a gift of God, by which we are enabled to comprehend the high mysteries of our Faith.

Q. 792. What is counsel?

A. It is a gift of God, by which we discover the frauds and deceits of the Devil, and are not deceived by him.

Q. 793. What is fortitude?

A. It is a gift of God, whereby we are enabled to undergo and despise all dangers for his sake.

Q. 794. What is knowledge?

A. It is a gift of God, by which we know and understand the will of God.

Q. 795. What is piety?

A. It is a gift of God, which makes us devout and zealous in his service.

Q. 796. What is the fear of the Lord?

A. It is the gift of God, which curbs our rashness, withholds us from sin, and makes us obedient to God's law.

# The Twelve Fruits of the Holy Ghost Expounded

Q. 797. How many are the fruits of the Holy Ghost?

A. There are twelve, as you may see, Gal. v. 22, 23.

Q. 798. What is the first?

A. Charity, whose nature and effects you know already.

Q. 799. What is the second?

A. Joy, by which we are enabled to serve God with cheerful hearts.

Q. 800. What is the third?

A. Peace, which keeps us unmoved in our minds amidst the storms and tempests of the world.

Q. 801. What is the fourth?

A. Patience, which enables us to suffer all adversities for the love of God.

Q. 802. What is the fifth?

A. Longanimity, which is an untired confidence of mind, in expecting the good things of the life to come.

Q. 803. What is the sixth?

A. Goodness, which makes us hurt no man, and be good to all.

Q. 804. What is the seventh?

A. Benignity, which causeth an affable sweetness in our manners and conversation.

Q. 805. What is the eighth?

A. Mildness, which allays in us all the [e]motions of passion and anger.

Q. 806. What is the ninth?

A. Fidelity, which makes us punctual observers of our covenants and promises.

Q. 807. What is the tenth?

A. Modesty, which observes a becoming deportment in all our outward actions.

Q. 808. What is the eleventh?

A. Continency, which makes us not only abstemious in meat and drink, but in all other sensible delights.

Q. 809. What is the twelfth?

A. Chastity, which keeps a pure soul in a pure body.

Q. 810. Who are they that have these fruits?

A. The children of God only; for "whosoever are led by the spirit of God, they are the sons of God." Rom. viii. 14.

# The Works of Mercy (corporal and spiritual) Expounded

Q. 811. How many are the corporal works of mercy?

A. Seven. 1. To feed the hungry. 2. To give drink to the thirsty. 3. To clothe the naked. 4. To harbour the harbourless. 5. To visit the sick. 6. To visit the imprisoned. 7. To bury the dead.

Q. 812. How prove you that these works are meritorious of a reward?

A. Because Christ hath promised the kingdom of Heaven as the reward of them. "Come, O ye blessed of my Father (saith he) and possess ye the kingdom, &c. for I was hungry, and ye gave me to eat," &c. Matt. xxv. 35, 36.

Q. 813. When are we said to feed and clothe Christ?

A. As often as we feed and clothe the poor, "What ye have done (saith he) to one of my little ones, that ye have done unto me." ver. 40.

Q. 814. Is the reward of these works a reward of justice?

A. It is; according to 2 Tim. iv. 7, 8. "I have fought a good fight (saith Paul) there is a crown of justice laid up for me, which our Lord will render to me at that day as the just judge."

Q. 815. What other proof have you?

A. Out of Heb. vi. 10. "For God is not unjust, that he should forget the work and love, which you have shown in his name, who have ministered unto the Saints, and do minister.

Q. 816. How many are the works of mercy, spiritual?

A. Seven also. 1. To give counsel to the doubtful. 2. To instruct the ignorant. 3. To admonish the sinners. 4. To comfort the afflicted. 5. To forgive offences. 6. To bear patiently the troublesome. 7. To pray for the quick and the dead.

Q. 817. How prove you your prayer for the dead?

A. First, out of the places before and after cited for purgatory. Secondly, out of 1 John v. 16. "He that knoweth his brother to sin a sin not unto death, let him ask, and life shall be given him, not sinning to death; (i.e.) to final impenitence. Therefore it is lawful to pray for all such as die penitent, confessing their sins." And in 2 Mac. xii. we read, "It is a wholesome and holy thought to pray for the dead, that they may be loosed from their sins."

Q. 818. How show you these works to be meritorious?

A. Out of Dan. xii. 3. "They who instruct others to justice, shall shine as stars to all eternity."

# The Eight Beatitudes

Q. 819. What are the eight Beatitudes?

A. Christ "opening his mouth he taught them, saying: 1. Blessed are the poor in spirit: for theirs is the kingdom of heaven. 2. Blessed are the meek, for they shall possess the land. 3. Blessed are they that mourn: for they shall be comforted. 4. Blessed are they that hunger and thirst after justice: for they shall be filled. 5. Blessed are the merciful: for they shall obtain mercy. 6. Blessed are the clean of heart: for they shall see God. 7. Blessed are the peace-makers: for they shall be called the children of God. 8. Blessed are they that suffer persecution for justice sake: for theirs is the Kingdom of heaven." Matt. v. 3, 10.

Q. 820. Whence ariseth the necessity of suffering persecution?

A. Because all that will live piously in Jesus Christ shall suffer persecution. 2 Tim. iii. 12.

# The Kinds of Sin Expounded

Q. 821. Why is it necessary for a Christian to know the nature and kinds of sin?

A. That so he may detest and avoid them.

Q. 822. How many kinds of sins are there?

A. Two, namely, Original and Actual.

Q. 823. What is original sin?

A. It is a privation of original justice, which we inherit from our first parent Adam, being all by course of nature, conceived and born in that privation or original sin.

Q. 824. How prove you that?

A. Out of Rom. v. 12. "Therefore as by one man sin entered into the world, and by sin death, and so unto all men death did pass, in whom all have sinned."

Q. 825. What are the effects of original sin?

A. Concupiscence, ignorance, evil inclination, proneness to sin, sickness, and death.

Q. 826. How is original sin taken away?

A. By holy baptism.

Q. 827. Whither go infants that die without baptism?

A. To a part of hell, where they endure the pain of loss, but not of sense, and shall never see the face of God.

Q. 828. How prove you that?

A. Out of John iii. 5. "Unless a man be born again of water, and the Holy Ghost, he cannot enter into the kingdom of God."

Q. 829. What is actual sin?

A. It is a thought, word or deed, contrary to the law of God.

Q. 830. What is the sin of omission?

A. To omit any thing willing, which is commanded by God or his Church.

Q. 831. Why is actual sin so called?

A. Because the material part of it is commonly some voluntary acts of ours.

Q. 832. Is all sin voluntary and deliberate?

A. It is, because (speaking of actual sin) no man sinneth in doing that which is not in his power to avoid.

Q. 833. What other proof have you?

A. Because the whole gospel of Christ is nothing else but an exhortation to do good, and avoid evil, than which nothing were more vain, if it be not the free election and power of man, assisted by God's grace, to do, or not to do such things.

Q. 834. What scripture have you for that?

A. First out of Gen. iv. 7. "If thou dost well, shalt thou not receive? But if ill, shall not thy sin be forthwith present at the door? But the lust thereof shall be under thee, and thou shalt have dominion over it."

Secondly out of Deut. xxx. 19, 20. "I call heaven and earth to witness this day, that I have proposed to thee life and death, blessing and cursing, choose therefore life that thou mayest live."

Thirdly, out of 1 Cor. vii. 37. "He that hath determined in his heart being settled not having necessity but having the power of his own will, and hath judged in his heart to keep his virginity, doth well;" (you see man hath power of his own will) and in Phil. iv. 13. "I can do all things (saith Paul) in him who strengtheneth me."

Q. 835. Doth not the efficacy of God's grace hinder, and hurt the freedom of our will?

A. No, it perfects it according to 1 Cor. xv. 10, 11. "I have laboured more abundantly (saith Paul) than all they, yet not I, but the grace of God within me." You hear the grace of God did not hinder, but perfect his working.

Q. 836. How is actual sin divided?

A. Into mortal and venial.

Q. 837. What is mortal sin?

A. And great offence against the love of God; and is so called because it kills the soul,

and robs it of the spiritual life of grace.

Q. 838. What is venial sin?

A. A small, and very pardonable offence against God, or our neighbour.

Q. 839. How prove you that some sins are mortal?

A. First, out of Rom. vi. 23. "For the wages of sin is death." And ver. xxi. "What fruit therefore had you then in these things, for which ye are now ashamed, for the end of them is death?"

Secondly, out of Wis. xvi. 14. "For man by malice, killeth his own soul." And out of Ezek. xviii. 4. "The soul that sinneth, the same shall die."

Q. 840. How prove you that some sins are venial?

A. First, out of 1 John i. 8, where speaking of such as walk in the light, and are cleansed from all mortal sin by the blood of Christ, he adds, "if we stay we have no sin, we seduce ourselves, and the truth is not in us."

Secondly, "In many things we all offend," James iii 2. And in Prov. xxiv. 16. "The just man falleth seven times." Not mortally, for then he were no longer just, therefore venially.

Thirdly, out of Matt. xii. 36. "But I say unto you, every idle word which men shall speak, they shall render an account for it at the day of judgment." Now God forbid every idle word should be a mortal sin.

Q. 841. What are the effects of venial sin?

A. It doth not rob the soul of life, as mortal sin doth, but only weakeneth the fervour of charity, and by degrees disposeth unto mortal.

Q. 842. Why are we bound to shun not only mortal, but venial sins?

A. Because "he that contemneth small things, shall fall by little and little." Eccles. xix. 1.

Q. 843. What other proof have you?

A. Because "no polluted thing shall enter into the heavenly Jerusalem." Apoc. xxi. 27, be it polluted with mortal, or venial sin.

Q. 844. How shall we be able to know when any sin is mortal, and when but venial?

A. Because to any mortal sin it is required, both that it be deliberate, and perfectly voluntary; and that it be a matter of weight against the law of God; one or both of which conditions are always wanting in a venial sin.

Q. 845. How is mortal sin remitted?

A. By hearty penance and contrition.

Q. 846. How is venial sin remitted?

A. By all the sacraments, by holy water, devout prayer, alms-deeds, and the like good works.

Q. 847. Whither go such as die in venial sin, or not having fully satisfied for the temporal punishments due to their mortal sins which are forgiven them?

A. To purgatory till they have made full satisfaction for them, and then to heaven.

Q. 848. How prove you there is a purgatory, or a place of punishment, where souls are purged after death?

Out of 1 Pet. iii. 10. "Christ being dead for our sins, came in spirit, and preached to them also that were in prison, who had been incredulous in the days of Noah, when the Ark was building."

Q. 849. What other proof have you?

A. Out of 1 Cor. iii. 13. "The work of every man shall be manifest, for the day of our Lord will declare it, because it shall be revealed in fire; and the work of every one of What kind it is, the fire shall try; If a man's work abides," (as theirs doth who deserve no purgatory) he shall suffer loss, but himself shall be saved, yet so as by fire."

Q. 850. What besides?

A. Out of Matt. v. 25. "Be thou at agreement with thy adversary betimes whilst thou art in the way with him (that is in this life) lest perhaps the adversary deliver thee to the judge, and the judge deliver thee to the officer, and thou be cast into prison (Purgatory): Amen, I say unto thee, thou shalt not go out from thence, till thou pay the last farthing."

Q. 851. What other yet?

A. Out of Matt. xii. 32. "Some sins shall neither be forgiven in this world, nor in the world to come." Therefore there is a place of purging and pardoning sins after this life.

Q. 852. How is a man made guilty, or said to co-operate to other men's sins?

A. As often as he is an actual cause of sin in others by any of these nine means: 1. By counsel. 2. By command. 3. By consent. 4. By provocation. 5. By praise or flattery. 6. By silence. 7. By connivance. 8. By participation; or 9. By defence of the ill done.

# The Seven Deadly Sins Expounded

Q. 853. How call you the seven deadly, or capital sins?

A. Pride, covetousness, lechery, anger, gluttony, envy, and sloth.

## Pride Expounded

Q. 854. What is pride?

A. It is an inordinate desire of our own excellency or esteem.

Q. 855. Why is pride called a capital sin?

A. Because it is the head or fountain of many other sins.

Q. 856. What for example?

A. Vain-glory, boasting, hypocrisy, ambition, arrogance, presumption, and contempt of others.

Q. 857. What is vain-glory?

A. And inordinate desire of human praise.

Q. 858. What is boasting?

A. A foolish bragging of ourselves.

Q. 859. What is hypocrisy?

A. Counterfeiting of more piety and virtue than we have.

Q. 860. What is ambition?

A. An inordinate desire of honour.

Q. 861. What is arrogance?

A. A high contempt of others, joined with insolence and rashness.

Q. 862. What is presumption?

A. An attempting of things above our strength.

Q. 863. What is contempt of others?

A. A disdainful preferring ourselves before others.

Q. 864. What other daughters hath pride?

A. Pertinency, discord, disobedience, and ingratitude.

Q. 865. What is pertinency?

A. A willful sticking to our own opinions, contrary to the judgment of our betters.

Q. 866. What is discord?

A. A wrangling in words, with such as we ought to assent and yield unto.

Q. 867. What is disobedience?

A. An opposition to the will or commands of parents and superiors.

Q. 868. What is ingratitude?

A. A forgetting or neglecting of benefits.

Q. 869. How prove you pride to be a mortal sin?

A. Because we read, that "God resists the proud, and gives this grace to the humble." 1 Pet. v. 5. And "pride is odious before God and men." Eccl. x. 7.

Q. 870. What are the remedies of pride?

A. To remember that holy lesson of Christ, "learn of me, because I am meek and humble of heart." Matt. xi. 29. And to consider that we are sinful dust and shall return again to dust; and that Whatsoever good we have to do, is the free gift of God.

Q. 871. What is the virtue opposite to pride?

A. Humility, which teaches us a lowly opinion of ourselves. "He that humbleth himself shall be exalted." Matt. xxiii. 12.

## Covetousness Expounded

Q. 872. What is covetousness?

A. An inordinate desire of riches.

Q. 873. When is covetousness a mortal sin?

A. When either we desire to get unjustly What which is another man's of considerable value, or else refuse to give of that which is our own, to such as are in any extreme or great necessity.

Q. 874. How prove you the first part?

A. Out of 1 Tim. vi. 9. "They, who would become rich, fall into temptation, and into the snare of the devil, and into many unprofitable and hurtful desires, which drown men in destruction and perdition: for covetousness is the root of all evils."

Q. 875. How prove you the latter part?

A. Out of 1 John iii. 17. "He that hath the substance of this world, and shall see his brother in necessity, and shall shut up his bowels from him; How doth the charity of God abide in him?"

Q. 876. What other proof have you for alms?

A. Out of Luke xi. 41. "But yet that which remains, give alms, and behold all things are clean unto you." And out of Dan. iv. 24. "Redeem thy sins with alms and thy iniquity with the mercies of the poor."

Q. 877. What are the daughters of covetousness?

A. Hardness of heart, unmercifulness to the poor unquiet solicitude, neglect of heavenly things, and confidence in things of this world.

Q. 878. What else?

A. Usury, fraud, rapine, theft, &c.

Q. 879. What are the remedies of covetousness?

A. To consider "that it is a kind of idolatry," according to Col. iii. 5. And that "it is harder for a rich man to enter into heaven, that for a camel to pass through the eye of a needle." Matt. xix. 24.

Q. 880. What are the virtues opposite to covetousness?

A. Liberality, which makes a man give freely to the poor; and justice, which renders to a men that which is theirs. "It is a more blessed thing thing to give (saith our Lord) than to take." Acts xxvi. 35. And 2 Cor. ix. 6, St. Paul saith, "He that soweth sparingly, sparingly also shall he reap; but he that soweth in blessings, of blessings also shall he reap; for God loves the cheerful giver."

# Lechery Expounded

Q. 881. What is lechery, or lust?

A. An inordinate desire of carnal sin, or delights of the flesh.

Q. 882. How prove you the malice of this sin?

A. Because the whole world was once drowned, and the cities of Sodom and Gemorrah were burnt with fire from heaven for it. Gen. vii. 21, and xix. 24.

Q. 883. What other proof have you?

A. Out of Rom. viii. 13. "For if you live according to the flesh, you shall die; but if by the spirit you mortify the deeds of the flesh, you shall live."

Q. 884. What are the degrees of lust?

A. Thought, delight, consent, and act.

Q. 885. What are the daughters of lust?

A. Fornication, whoredom, adultery, voluntary pollution, unchaste signs and touches, wanton kisses and speeches.

Q. 886. How prove you voluntary pollution to be a mortal sin?

A. Out of Gen. xxxviii. 9, where we read, that Onan was struck dead by God in the place, for shedding the seed of nature out of the due use of marriage to hinder generation, which fact the holy text calls a destestable thing. He also who was eldest brother to this Onan, was slain by God, as we read in the same chapter, ver. 7. And it is generally thought by expositors, that his sudden death was in punishment for the like sin of pollution.

Q. 887. Why are the lustful kisses and touches mortal sins?

A. Because they vehemently dispose to fornication and pollution.

Q. 888. Is kissing by way of civility, when we meet friend, any sin?

A. No, it is not.

Q. 889. What are the remedies of lust?

A. To consider the beastliness of it, and that by it we make our bodies, which are members of Christ, to be members of an harlot. 1 Cor. vi. 15.

Q. 890. What else?

A. To consider that God and his angels are even witnesses of it, How private soever it may seem.

Q. 891. What if the virtue opposite to lechery?

A. Chastity, which makes us abstain from carnal pleasures. "Let us behave ourselves (saith St. Paul) as the ministers of God, in much patience, in watching, in fasting, in chastity." 2 Cor. vi. 4, 6.

Q. 892. How prove you the greatness of this virtue?

A. Out of Apoc. xiv. 4. "These are they who were not defiled with women, for they are virgins, these follow the Lamb withersoever he shall go."

## Envy Expounded

Q. 893. What is envy?

A. It is a sadness or repining at another's good, in as much as it seems to lessen our own excellency.

Q. 894. How prove you envy to be a mortal sin?

A. Because, by the "Devil's envy death entered into the world, and envy was the cause of all sin." Wis. ii. 24.

Q. 895. What are the daughters of envy?

A. Hatred, detraction, rash judgment, strife, reproach, contempt, and rejoicing at another's evil.

Q. 896. What are the remedies of envy?

A. To consider that it robs us of charity, and deforms us to the likeness of the Devil.

Q. 897. What is the opposite to envy?

A. Brotherly love, which is the chiefest badge of Christianity, "In this all men should know that you are my disciples, if you love one another." John xiii. 35.

## Gluttony Expounded

Q. 898. What is gluttony?

A. An inordinate excess, or desire of excess in meat or drink.

Q. 899. How prove you that to be a mortal sin?

A. Out of Cor. vi. 10. "Drunkards shall not possess the kingdom of God." And Luke xxi.

34. "Take heed to yourselves, lest your hearts be overcharged with surfeiting and drunkenness."

Q. 900. What are the daughters of gluttony?

A. Babbling scurrility, spewing, sickness, and dullness of soul and body.

Q. 901. What are the remedies of it.

A. To consider the abstinence of Christ and his Saints, and that "gluttons are enemies to the cross of Christ, whose end is destruction." Phil. iii. 19.

## Anger Expounded

Q. 902. What is anger?

A. An inordinate desire of revenge.

Q. 903. How prove you anger to be mortal?

A. Out of Matt. ver. 22. "Whosoever shall be angry with his brother, shall be guilty of judgment, &c. And whosoever shall say, thou fool, shall be guilty of hell fire."

Q. 904. What are the daughters of anger?

A. Hatred, passion, fury, clamour, threats, contumey, cursing, blasphemy, and murder.

Q. 905. What are the remedies of anger?

A. To remember the holy lesson of Christ, Luke xxi. 19. "In your patience you shall possess your souls." And that of St. Paul. "Be gentle one to another, pardoning one another, as also God in Christ hath pardoned you." Ephes. iv. 32.

Q. 906. What is the virtue opposite to anger?

A. Patience, which suppresseth in us all passion, and desire of revenge.

Q. 907. How prove you the necessity and force of patience?

A. Out of Heb. x. 36. "Patience is necessary for you, that doing the will of God, you may partake of the promise."

## Sloth Expounded

Q. 908. What is sloth?

A. Laziness of mind, neglecting to begin, or prosecute good things.

Q. 909. How prove you sloth to be a deadly sin?

A. Out of Apoc. iii. 15. "Because thou art neither cold nor hot, but lukewarm, I will begin to cast thee out of my mouth."

Q. 910. What other proof have you?

A. Out of Matt. xxv. 30. "And the unprofitable servant cast ye forth into exterior darkness."

Q. 911. When is sloth mortal?

A. As often as by it we break any commandment of God or his church.

Q. 912. What are daughters of sloth?

A. Tepidity, pusillanimity, indevotion, weariness of life, aversion from spiritual things, and distrust of God's mercy.

Q. 913. What are the remedies of sloth?

A. To remember that of Jeremiah xlvii. 10. "Cursed be he that doth the work of the Lord negligently." And to consider with What diligence men do worldly business.

Q. 914. What is the virtue opposite to sloth?

A. Diligence, which makes us careful and zealous to performing our duty both to God and men. "Take heed, watch and pray, for you know not when the time is," Matt. Xiii. 33. "Strive to enter by the narrow gate, for many I say to you, shall seek to enter, and shall not be able." Luke xiii. 24.

# The Sins against the Holy Ghost Expounded

Q. 915. How many are the sins against the Holy Ghost?

A. Six: despair of salvation, presumption of God's mercy, to impugn the known truth, envy at another's spiritual good, obstinacy in sin, and final impenitence.

Q. 916. What is despair of salvation?

A. It is a diffidence in the mercies and power of God as also, in the merits of Jesus Christ, as if they were not of force enough to save us. This was the sin of Cain, when he said, "My sin is greater than I can deserve pardon." Gen. iv. 13. And of Judas, "when casting down the silver pieces in the temple, he went and hanged himself." Matt. xxvii. 4, 5.

Q. 917. What is the presumption of God's mercy?

A. A foolish confidence of salvation, without leading a good life, or any care to keep the commandments; such as they entertain who think they will be saved by faith only, without good works.

Q. 918. What is it to impugn the known truth?

A. To argue obstinately against known points of faith, or to prevent the way of our Lord by forging lies and slander, as Heretics do, when they teach the ignorant people, that Catholics worship images as God, and give Angels and Saints the honour which is due to God; or that the Pope for money gives us pardon to commit What sins we please; that all which, greater falsehoods cannot be invented.

Q. 919. What is the envy to another's spiritual good?

A. A sadness or repining at another's growth in virtue and perfection; such as sectaries seem to have when they scoff and are troubled at the frequent fasts, prayers, feasts, pilgrimages, alms-deeds, vows, and religious orders of the Catholic Church, calling them superstitious and fooleries, because they have not in their churches any such practices of piety.

Q. 920. What is obstinacy in sin?

A. A wilful persisting in wickedness, and running on from sin to sin, after sufficient instructions and admonition.

Q. 921. How show you the malice of this sin?

A. Out of Heb. x. 26, 27. "If we sin wilfully after having received the knowledge of the truth, there is now left no sacrifice for sins, but a certain dreadful expectation of judgment."

Q. 922. What other proof have you?

A. Out of 2 Pet. ii. 21. "It was better for them not to know the way of justice, than after the knowledge to turn back from the holy commandment which was given them."

Q. 923. What is final impenitence?

A. To die without either confession or contrition for our sins, as those do of whom it is said, "With a hard neck, and with uncircumcised hearts and ears, you always resist the Holy Ghost." Acts vii. 51. And in the person of whom Job speaks, saying, "Depart thou from us, and we will not have the knowledge of thy ways." Job xxi. 14.

Q. 924. Why is it said that those sins should never be forgiven, neither in this world, nor in the world to come?

A. Not because there is no power in God or in the sacraments to remit them, if we confess them, and be sorry for them, (excepting only final impenitence) of which we read, "There is a sin to death for that I say not that any man ask." 1 John i. 9. "If we confess our sins, he is faithful and just to forgive our sins, and cleanse us from all iniquity."

# The Sins that cry to Heaven for Vengeance Expounded

Q. 925. How many such sins are there?

A. Four.

Q. 926. What is the first of them?

A. Wilful murder, which is a voluntary and unjust taking away another's life.

Q. 927. How show you the pravity of this sin?

A. Out of Gen. iv. 10. Where it is said to Cain "What hast thou done? the voice of the blood of thy brother crieth to me from the earth: now, therefore shalt thou be cursed upon the earth." And Matt. xxvi 52, "All that take the sword, shall perish with the sword."

Q. 928. What is the second?

A. The sin of Sodom, or carnal sin against nature, which is a voluntary shedding of the seed of nature, out of the due use of marriage, or lust with a different sex.

Q. 929. What is the scripture proof of this?

A. Out of Gen. xix. 13. where we read of the Sodomites, and their sin. "We will destroy this place because the cry of them hath increased before our Lord, who hath sent us to destroy them," (and they were burnt with fire from heaven.)

Q. 930. What is the third?

A. Oppressing of the poor, which is a cruel, tyrannical, and unjust dealing with inferiors.

Q. 931. What other proof have you of that?

A. Out of Exod. xxii. 21. "Ye shall not hurt the widow and the fatherless: If you do hurt them, they will cry unto me, and I will hear them cry, and my fury shall take indignation, and I will strike thee with the sword." And out of Isa. x. 1, 2. "Wo to them that make unjust laws, that they might oppress the poor in judgment, and do violence to the cause of the humble of my people."

Q. 932. What is the fourth?

A. To defraud working men of their wages, which is to lessen, or detain it from them.

Q. 933. What proof have you of it?

A. Out of Eccl. xxxiv. 37. "He that sheddeth blood and he that defraudeth the hired man, are brethren," and out of James v. 4. "Behold the hire of the workmen that have reaped your fields, which is defrauded by you, crieth, and their cry hath entered into the ears of the Lord God of Sabaoth."

# The Four Last Things Expounded

Q. 934. What are the four last things?

A. Death, Judgment, Hell, and Heaven.

Q. 935. What understand you by death?

A. That we are mortal, and shall once die; How soon, we are uncertain, and therefore we must be always prepared for it.

Q. 936. How prove you that?

A. Out of Heb. ix. 27. "It is decreed for all men once to die." And Matt. xxv. 13. "Watch ye therefore, because ye know not the day nor the hour."

Q. 937. What is the best preparation for death?

A. A godly life, and to be often doing penance for our sins, and saying with St. Paul, "I desire to be dissolved and to be with Christ." Phil. i. 23.

Q. 938. What else?

A. To remember often that of Matt. xvi. 25. "He that will save his life shall lose it, and he that shall lose his life for me shall find it."

Q. 939. What understand you by judgment?

A. I understand, that (besides the general judgment at the last day) our souls as soon as we are dead, shall receive their particular judgment at the tribunal of Christ, according to that, "Blessed are the dead that die in the Lord, from henceforth now, saith the spirit, they rest from their labours, for their works follow them." Apoc. xiv. 13.

Q. 940. What is the best preparation from this judgment?

A. To remember often that of Heb. x. 31. It is a terrible thing to fall into the hands of the living God." And that of 1 Cor. xi. 21. "For if we did judge our selves, we should not be judged."

Q. 941. What understand you by hell?

A. That such as die in mortal sin "shall be tormented there both day and night, and for ever and ever." Apoc. xx. 21. "There shall be weeping, Howling, and gnashing of teeth; the worm of conscience shall always gnaw them, and the fire that torments them, shall never be extinguished." Mark viii. 44, 45.

Q. 942. What understand you by heaven?

A. That the elect and faithful servants of God, shall for ever reign with him in hiskingdom, "where he hath such delights and comforts for them, as neither eye hath seen or ear hath heard, neither hath it entered into the heart of man." 1 Cor. ii. 9.

Q. 943. How prove you that?

A. Out of Matt. vii. 21. "He hath doth the will of my Father who is in heaven, shall enter into the kingdom of heaven."

Q. 944. What profit is there in the frequent memory of all those things?

A. Very great according to that, "In all thy works remember the last things, and thou shalt never sin." Eccles. vii. 40. which God of his great mercy give us grace to do. Amen.

# The Substance or Essence, and Ceremonies of the Mass, Expounded

Q. 945. What is the mass?

A. It is the unbloody sacrifice of Christ's body and blood, under the forms of bread and wine. The word Mass, used in English, being derived from Missa, Latin;

143

and the word Missa, though it may have other derivations, may be well taken from the Hebrew word Missach, which signifies a free voluntary offering.

Q. 946. Who instituted the substance or essence of the Mass?

A. Our Saviour Christ at his last supper, when he consecrated, i.e. converted the substance of bread and wine into his own true body and blood, and gave the same to his disciples, under the outward forms of bread and wine, commanding them to do What he had done in commemoration of him. Luke xxii. 19.

Q. 947. Who ordained the ceremonies of the mass?

A. The church, directed by the Holy Ghost.

Q. 948. For What end did the church ordain them?

A. To stir up devotion in the people, and reverence to the sacred mysteries.

Q. 949. For What other end?

A. To instruct the ignorant in spiritual and high things by sensible and material signs; and by the glory of the church militant to make them comprehend something of the glory of the triumphant church.

Q. 950. What warrant hath the church to ordain ceremonies?

A. The authority of God himself in the old law, commanding many and most stately ceremonies in things belonging to his service. See the whole book of Leviticus.

Q. 951. What besides?

A. The example of Christ in the new law using dust and spittle to cure the blind, the deaf, and dumb. He prostrated himself at prayer in the garden three times. He lifted up his eyes to heaven and groaned, when he was raising Lazarus from the dead, which were all ceremonies.

Q. 952. Did he use any ceremonies at the last supper, where he ordained the sacrifice of the mass?

144

A. He did; for he washed the feet of his disciples, he blessed the bread and the cup, and exhorted the communicants.

Q. 953. What signify the several ornaments of the priest?

A. The Amict, or linen veil, which he first puts on, represents the veil with which the Jews covered the face of Christ, when they buffeted him in the house of Caiaphas, and bid him prophesy, "who it was that struck him."

2. The Alb signifies the white garment, which Herod put on him, to intimate that he was a fool.

3. The Girdle signifies the cord that bound him in the garden.

4. The Maniple, the cord which bound him to the pillar.

5. The Stole, the cord by which they led him to the crucified.

6. The priest's upper, Vestment, represents both the seamless coat of Christ, as also the purple garment with which they clothed him in derision in the house of Pilate.

7. The Altar-stone, represents the cross on which he offered himself unto the Father.

8. The Chalice, the sepulchre or grave of Christ.

9. The Paten, the stone which was rolled to the door of the sepulchre.

10. The Altar-cloths, with the corporal and Pall, the linen in which the dead body of Christ was shrouded and buried. Finally, the candles on the Altar puts us in mind of the light which Christ brought into the world by his passion, as also of his immortal and ever shining divinity.

Q. 954. What meaneth the priest's coming back three steps from the Altar, and humbling himself before he begins?

A. It signifies the prostrating of Christ in the garden, when he began his passion.

Q. 955. Why doth the priest bow himself again at the Confiteor?

A. To move the people to humiliation; and to signify that by the merits and passion of Christ, (which they are there to commemorate) salvation may be had, if it be sought with a contrite and humble heart.

Q. 956. Why doth he beat his breast as Mea Culpa?

A. To teach the people to return into the heart, and signifies that all sin is from the heart, and ought to be discharged from the heart, with hearty sorrow.

Q. 957. Why doth the priest, ascending to the Altar, kiss it in the middle?

A. Because the Altar signifies the church, composed of divers people, as of divers living stones, which Christ kissed in the middle, by giving a holy kiss of peace and unity, both to the Jews and Gentiles.

Q. 958. What signifies the Introit?

A. It is, as it were, the entrance into the office, or that which the priest saith first after his coming to the Altar, and signifies the desires and groanings of the ancient fathers longing for the coming Christ.

Q. 959. Why is the Introit repeated twice?

A. To signify the frequent repetition of their desires and supplications.

Q. 960. Why do we add unto the Introit, Gloria Patri, &c. glory be to the Father, &c. Amen?

A. To render thanks to the most Blessed Trinity for our redemption, accomplished by the cross.

Q. 961. What means the Kyrie Eleison?

A. It signifies, "Lord have mercy on us," and is repeated thrice in honour of the Son, and thrice in honour of the Holy Ghost.

Q. 962. Why so often?

A. To signify our great necessity, and earnest desires to find mercy.

Q. 963. It signifies, "Glory be to God on high;" and is the song which the angels sung at the birth of Christ, used in this place to signify, that the mercy which we beg, was brought us by the birth and death of Christ.

Q. 964. What means the Oremus?

A. It signifies, "Let us pray;" and is the priest's address to the people, by which he invites them to join with him, both in his prayer and intention.

Q. 965. What means the Collect?

A. It is the priest's prayer, and is called a Collect, because it collects and gathers together the supplications of the multitude, speaking them all with one voice and also because it is a collection, or sum of the Epistle and Gospel, for the most part of the year, especially of all the Sundays.

Q. 966. Why doth the clerk say, Amen.

A. He doth it in the name of the people, to signify, that all concur with the priest, in his petition of prayer.

Q. 967. What meaneth the Dominus Vobiscum?

A. It signifies, "Our Lord be with you," and is used to beg God's presence and assistance to the people, in the performance of that work.

Q. 968. Why is it answered Et cum Spiritu tuo, "and with thy spirit?"

A. To signify, that the people with one consent do beg the like for him.

Q. 969. Why are all the prayers ended with Per Dominum nostrum Jesum Christum, &c. "Through our Lord Jesus Christ?"

A. To signify, that Whatsover we beg of God the Father, we must beg it in the name of Jesus Christ, by whom he hath given us all things.

Q. 970. What signifies the Epistle?

A. It signifies the old law; as also the preaching of the Prophets and the Apostles, out of whom it is commonly taken: and it is read before the Gospel, to intimate that the old law being able to bring nothing to perfection, it was necessary the new should succeed it.

Q. 971. What means the Gradual?

A. It signifies the penance preached by St. John Baptist, and that we cannot obtain the salvation of Christ, but by the holy degrees of penance.

Q. 972. What means the Alleluiah?

A. It is the voice of men rejoicing, and aspiring to the joys of heaven.

Q. 973. Why is the Alleluiah repeated so often at the feast of Easter?

A. Because it is the joyful solemnity of our Saviour's resurrection.

Q. 974. Why between the Septuagesima and Easter, is the Tract read in the place of the Gradual?

A. Because it is a time of penance and mourning, and therefore the Tract is read with a mournful and slow voice, to signify the miseries and punishments of this life.

Q. 975. What is the Tract?

A. Two or three versicles between the Epistle and the Gospel, sung with a slow, long protracted tone.

Q. 976. Why do we rise up at the reading of the Gospel?

A. To signify our readiness to go, and do, whither, and Whatsoever it commands us.

Q. 977. What means the Gospel?

A. It signifies the preaching of Christ; and is the happy embassy or message of Christ unto the world.

Q. 978. Why is the Gospel read at the North end, or left side of the Altar?

A. To signify that by the preaching of the Gospel of Christ, the kingdom of the Devil was overthrown.

Q. 979. How prove you that?

A. Because the Devil hath chosen the North (figuratively infidels, and the wicked) for the seat of his malice. "From the North shall all evil be opened upon all the inhabitants of the land." Jer. i. 14. and Zach. ii. 7.

Q. 980. Why doth the priest before he begins the Gospel, salute the people with Dominus vobiscum?

A. To prepare them for a devout hearing of it, and to beg of our Lord to make them worthy hearers of his word, which can save their souls.

Q. 981. Why then doth he say, Sequentia sancti Evangelii, &c. The sequel of the Holy Gospel, &c.?

A. To move attention, and to signify What part of the Gospel he then reads.

Q. 982. Why doth the clerk answer, Gloria tibi Domine, Glory be to thee, O Lord?

A. To give the glory of the gospel to God, who hath of his mercy made us partakers of it.

Q. 983. Why then doth the priest sign the book with the sign of the cross?

A. To signify that the doctrine there delivered, appertains to the cross and passion of Christ.

Q. 984. Why after this do both priest and people sign themselves with the cross in three places?

A. They sign themselves on their foreheads, to signify they are not, nor will be ashamed to profess Christ crucified: on their mouths to signify they will be ready with their mouths, to confess unto salvation: and on their breast to signify that with their hearts they believe unto justice.

Q. 985. Why at the end of the Gospel, do they sign their breast again with the sign of the cross?

A. That the Devil may not steal the seed of God's word out of their hearts.

Q. 986. What means the Creed?

A. It is a public profession of out faith, and the wholesome fruit of preaching the Gospel.

Q. 987. What means the first offertory, where the priest offers bread and wine mingled with water?

A. It signifies the freedom wherewith Christ offered himself in his whole life unto his passion, and the desire he had to suffer for our sins.

Q. 988. What signifies the mingling of water with wine?

A. It signifies the blood and water flowing from the side of Christ; as also the union of the faithful with Christ.

Q. 989. Why then doth the priest wash the ends of his fingers?

A. To admonish both himself and the people to wash away the unclean thoughts of their hearts, that so they may partake of that clean sacrifice: As also to signify, that the priest is, ought to be clean from mortal sin.

Q. 990. Why then after some silence, doth he begin the preface with an elevated voice, saying Per omnia sæcula sæculorum?

A. To signify the triumphant entry of Christ into Jerusalem, after he had lain hid a little space; and therefore it is ended with Hosana, benedictus qui venit, &c. which was the Hebrew children's song.

Q. 991. What else meaneth the preface?

A. It is a preparation of the people, for the approaching action of the sacrifice; and therefore the priest saith, Sursum corda, lift your hearts to God; so to move them to lay aside all earthly thoughts, and to think only on heavenly things.

Q. 992. Why at these words, Benedictus qui venit, Blessed is he that cometh in our Lord's name, doth he sign himself with the sign of the cross?

A. To signify that the entry of Christ into Jerusalem was not to a kingdom of this world, but to a death upon the cross.

Q. 993. What is the Canon?

A. It is a most sacred, essential, and substantial part of the mass, because in it the sacrifice is effected.

Q. 994. Why is the Canon read with a low voice?

A. To signify the sadness in our Saviour's passion, which is there effectually represented.

Q. 995. Why doth the priest begin the Canon bowing his head?

A. To signify the obedience of Christ unto his Father in making himself a sacrifice to sin.

Q. 996. What meaneth the Te-igitur, clementissime Pater, &c. Thee therefore, O most clement Father, &c.?

A. It is a humble and devout supplication to God our heavenly Father, made in the name of all the people, that he would vouchsafe to accept and bless the sacrifice which we are offering unto him for the peace, unity and conversation of the whole Catholic Church, and likewise for the Pope, our prelate, and all the other the truly faithful.

Q. 997. Why in the middle of this prayer doth the priest kiss the altar, and sign the Host and Chalice thrice with the sign of the cross?

A. He kisseth the altar, to show the kiss of peace which Christ gave us, by reconciling us to God in his own blood. He signeth the Host and Chalice thrice to signify that our redemption made upon the Cross, was done by the will of the Holy Trinity.

Q. 998. What meaneth the Memento Domine famulorum famularumque tuarum: Remember, O Lord, thy servants, men and women, &c.?

A. It is a commemoration of the living, in which the pries remembers by name, such as he intends chiefly to say mass for, and then in general, all present and all the faithful, beseeching God by virtue of the sacrifice, to bless them, and be mercifully mindful of them.

Q. 999. What means the Communicantes and memorum venerantes, &c. Communicating and worshipping the memory, &c.?

A. It is an exercise of our communion with the saints in which having recounted the names of the blessed virgin Mary, and many other glorious saints, we beg of God by their merits and intercession, to grant us the assistance of his protection in all things.

Q. 1000. What signifies the Hanc igitur oblationem, this offering therefore of our servitude, &c. when the priest spreads his hands over the Host and Chalice?

A. It is an earnest begging of God to accept the sacrifice that is presented to be offered for the safety and peace of the whole church, and salvation of all from eternal damnation.

Q. 1001. Why then doth he sign the offerings again five times?

A. To signify the mystery of those five days which were between our Saviour's entry into Jerusalem and his passion.

Q. 1002. What meaneth Qui pridie quam pateretur, who the day before he suffered, &c.

A. It is but a repetition and representation of What Christ did at his last supper, where he took bread, blessed it, &c. and immediately precedes the words of consecration spoken by the priest, by which he sacrificeth to God.

Q. 1003. What are the words of consecration?

A. "Hoc est corpus meum. &c. This is my body; This is the cup of my blood, of the New and eternal Testament; a mystery of faith, which shall be shed for you, and for the many, to the remission of sins." Matt. xxvi. 27, 28.

Q. 1004. What meaneth these words?

A. They signify according to the letter, What they effect and cause, viz. a change of the bread and wine into the body and blood of Christ; and in a mystery also they signify, unto us the incarnation, passion, resurrection, and ascension of Christ.

Q. 1005. Why after consecration of the Host, doth the priest kneel and adore?

A. He kneels and adores, to give sovereign honour to Christ, and signify the real presence of his body and blood in the blessed sacrament which he then holds in his hand.

152

Q. 1006. Why after consecration of the wine, doth the priest kneel and adore, saying, Hæc quotiescumque feceritis, &c. that is, "As often as you shall do these things, you shall do them in remembrance of me." 1 Cor. xi. 25?

A. He kneels and adores, to give sovereign honour to Christ, and to signify the real presence of Christ's body and blood in the chalice, then on the altar, and he speaks these words to signify, that as often as we say, or hear mass, and offer up this sacrifice, we must do it as Christ hath commanded us, in memory of his passion, resurrection and ascension: and therefore he goes on, beseeching God by all those mysteries, to look propitiously upon our holy and immaculate host, as he did upon the sacrifices of Abraham, Abel, and Melchisedech, and to replenish all that partake thereof, with heavenly grace and benediction.

Q. 1007. Why after consecration of each, doth the priest elevate, or lift up the consecrated host and chalice?

A. That all the people may adore the body and blood of Christ, as also to signify, that for our sins his body was lifted on the Cross and his blood shed.

Q. 1008. For What other end doth he elevate the host and chalice?

A. That he, with the whole multitude, may make oblations of Christ's body and blood unto God, which after consecration, is one of the most essential parts of the whole service of the mass, and signifies that oblation, wherewith Christ offered himself unto God upon the altar of the Cross.

Q. 1009. Why then doth he again sign the offerings five times with the sign of the Cross?

A. To signify the five wounds of Christ, which he represents to the eternal Father for us.

Q. 1010. What means the Momento?

A. It is a commemoration of the dead; in which the pries first nominates those whom he intends especially to apply the sacrifice unto; and then prays in general for all the faithful departed, beseeching God by virtue of that sacrifice, to give them rest, refreshment, and everlasting life.

Q. 1011. Why after the Momento for the dead, doth the priest elevate or raise his voice, saying, Nobis quoque peccatoribus, "and to us sinners also," &c.?

A. In memory of the supplication of the penitent thief made to Christ on the Cross; that so we also (though unworthy sinners) by the virtue of the sacrifice, may with him and the holy saints, be made partakers of the heavenly kingdom.

Q. 1012. Why then doth he again sign the Host and Chalice three times with the sign of the Cross?

A. To signify, that this sacrifice is available for three sorts of men: for those in heaven, to the increase or glory; for those in purgatory, to free up them from their pains; and for those on earth, to an increase of grace and remission of their sins; as also to signify the three hours which Christ did hang living upon the Cross, and all the griefs he sustained in them.

Q. 1013. Why then, uncovering the chalice, doth he sign it five times with the Host?

A. His uncovering the chalice is to signify, that at the death of Christ the veil of the temple was rent asunder. The three crosses made over the chalice, signify the three hours which Christ hung dead on the cross; the other two made at the brim of the chalice, signifying the blood and water flowing from his side.

Q. 1014. Why is the Pater Noster said with a loud voice?

A. To signify, by the seven petitions thereof, the seven mystical words which Christ spoke upon the Cross with a loud voice, viz. "Father, forgive them, they know not What they do. 2. To day shalt thou be with me in Paradise. 3. Behold thy mother; woman behold thy son. 4. My God, my God, Why hast thou forsaken me. 5. I thirst. 6. Into thy hands I commend my spirit. 7. It is consummated."

Q. 1015. What means the priest laying down the Host upon the corporal, and then covering the chalice again?

A. It signifies the taking of our Saviour down from the Cross, and his burial.

Q. 1016. Why, then is the priest silent for a time?

A. To signify our Saviour's rest in the sepulchre on the Sabbath?

Q. 1017. Why is the Host divided into three parts?

A. To signify the division of our Saviour's soul and body made on the Cross, and that the body was broken, and divided in three principle parts, namely his hands, side, and feet.

Q. 1018. Why after this doth he sign the chalice three times with a particle of the Host, and raise his voice saying, Pax Domini, &c., The peace of our Lord be always with you?

A. To signify that the frequent voice of Christ to his disciples, Pax vobis, Peace be to you; as also to signify the triple peace which he hath purchased for us, by his Cross, namely, external, internal, and eternal.

Q. 1019. Why then is the particle of the Host put into the chalice?

A. To signify the reuniting of our Saviour's body, blood and soul, made at his resurrection; as also to signify, that we cannot partake of the blood and merits of Christ, unless we partake of his cup of sufferings.

Q. 1020. Why is the Agnus Dei, or Lamb of God, which taketh away the sins of the world, said with a loud voice?

A. To commemorate the glory of our Saviour's ascension, and to signify that he was slainlike an innocent lamb to take away our sins and give us peace.

Q. 1021. Why is the Pax, or kiss of peace, given before communion?

A. To signify, that peace and mutual charity, which ought to be among the faithful, who all eat of one bread and of the Eucharist and are all members of one mystical body.

Q. 1022. What means the three prayers said by the priest before the communion?

A. They are said in honour of the blessed Trinity. In the first he begs peace for the whole church, and perfect charity among all Christians. In the second, he beseecheth God, by the body and blood of Christ, (which he is there about to receive) to free him from all evil. In the third, that it may not prove to his damnation and judgment, by an unworthy receiving of it, but to the defence and safety of his soul and body. And this immediately precedes the consummation of the Host and Chalice, which is another of the most essential parts of the whole service of the mass.

Q. 1023. What signifies the consummation of communion?

A. It signifies Christ's burial, and the consummation of his passion.

Q. 1024. What means the Domine non sum dignus, &c.?

A. It signifies, "O Lord, I am not worthy that thou shouldest enter under my roof; but only say the word," &c. And it was the Centurion's prayer, by which he obtained health for the sick boy, Matt. viii. 8. And teacheth us not to approach this sacrifice, but with an humble and contrite heart.

Q. 1025. What means the prayers said by the priest after communion?

A. They are thanksgiving to God for having made us partakers of his unbloody sacrifice of the Altar, and by it also of the bloody sacrifice of the Cross.

Q. 1026. What means the words Ite Missa est?

A. They signify, that the Host is offered, Mass ended, and the people dismissed; representing the voice of the angel dismissing the apostles and disciples when they stood looking up after Christ ascended into heaven, with, "O ye men of Galilee, Why stand you here looking up into heaven?" Acts i. 11.

Q. 1027. What means the priest lifting up his hands and blessing the people?

A. It signifies the blessing which Christ gave his apostles and disciples at his ascension, with his hands lifted up.

Q. 1028. What signifies the Gospel of St. John?

A. It signifies the Apostles preaching the gospel to all nations. Luke xxiv. 50.

Q. 1029. What is the missal?

A. It is the Mass book, wherein this holy service is contained.

# The Primer or Office of our Blessed Lady, Expounded

Q. 1030. Who composed this office?

A. The church, directed by the Holy Ghost.

Q. 1031. Why is the Primer so called?

A. From the Latin word Primo, which signifies, first of all, so to teach us, that prayer should be the first work of the day, according to that, "Seek ye first the kingdom of
heaven, and all these things shall be given you.

Q. 1032. Why is the office divided into Hymns, Psalms, Canticles, Antiphons, Versicles, Responsories, and Prayers?

A. For order, beauty, and variety sake.

Q. 1033. What warrant have you for that?

A. Out of Col. iii. 16. "Sing ye in your hearts unto the Lord in spiritual Psalms, Hymns, and Canticles."

Q. 1034. Why should the laity pray out of the Psalms, which they little understand?

A. 1. Because, by so doing, they pray out of the mouth of the Holy Ghost. 2. Because, if they do it with devout and humble hearts, it is as meritorious in them, as in the greatest scholars; for a petition hath the same force, whether it be delivered by a learned or unlearned man; so hath also prayer. 3. Because a psalm is of the same value in the sight of God, in the mouth of a child, or woman, as from the mouth of the most learned doctor.

Q. 1035. Why is the office divided into seven several hours?

A. That so it might be a daily memorial of the seven principal parts, and seven hours of our Saviour's passion.

Q. 1036. What ground have you for that?

A. Out of Zac. xii 10. "At that day I will pour out upon the house of David, and the inhabitants of Jerusalem, the spirit of grace and prayer, and they shall look up at him whom they have pierced."

Q. 1037. What meaneth at that day?

A. The day of grace, the new law.

Q. 1038. What means the house of David, and the inhabitants of Jerusalem?

A. The church of Christ.

Q. 1039. What means the spirit of grace and prayer?

A. The Holy Ghost which dictated the office, and poureth forth the grace of God into our souls by virtue of it.

Q. 1040. What means, "And they shall look up at him whom they have pierced?"

A. It signifies that the whole order, scope, and object of the office should be Christ crucified.

Q. 1041. How are the seven hours a memorial of the passion of Christ?

A. Because the seven hours were consumed in his passion; for three hours he hung living on the Cross; other three hours he hung dead upon it; and the seventh hour was spent in nailing him to and taking him from the cross.

Q. 1042. What do we commemorate by the Matins and Lauds?

A. His bloody sweat in the garden; as also his been dragged thence to Jerusalem.

Q. 1043. What by the prime or first hour?

A. The scoffs and indignations which he sustained, whilst they led him through the streets early in the morning to the princes of the Jews; as also the false accusations which then were brought against him.

Q. 1044. What by the third hour?

A. His whipping at the pillar, his crowning with thorns, his clothing with a purple garment, his sceptre of a reed, and showing to the people with these words: Behold the man.

Q. 1045. What by the sixth hour?

A. His unjust condemnation to death, his carrying the Cross, his stripping and nailing to the Cross.

Q. 1046. What by the ninth hour?

A. His drinking gall and vinegar, his dying on the Cross, and the opening his side with a spear.

Q. 1047. What by the even-song?

A. His taking down from the Cross, and the darkness which was made upon the face of the earth.

Q. 1048. What by the Complin?

A. His funeral and burial.

Briefly thus; The matins and lauds, his agony, and binding in the garden; the crime, his scoffs, and false accusations; the third hour, his clothing with purple, and crowning with  thorns; the sixth hour, his condemning and nailing to the Cross; the ninth hour, his  yielding up the ghost, and the opening his side; the even-song, his taking from the Cross; and the complin, his burial.

# The Particulars of the Office Expounded

Q. 1049. Why doth our Lady's office always begin with an Ave Maria?

159

A. To dedicate the office of our Lady, and to beg her aid for the devout performance of it to God's honour.

Q. 1050. Why do we begin every hour with, Incline unto my aid, O God: O Lord, make haste to help me?

A. To acknowledge our infirmity and misery, and out great need of divine assistance, not only in all other things, but also in our very prayers; according to that of the Apostles, "No man can say Lord Jesus, but in the Holy Ghost."

Q. 1051. Why do we add to this, Glory be to the Father, and to the Son, and to the Holy Ghost?

A. To signify that the intention of the office is, in the first place, to give one and equal glory to the most blessed Trinity, and to invite all creatures to do the like, this is the principle aim of the whole office; therefore we not only begin every hour, but also end every Psalm with the same verse.

Q. 1052. Who ordained the Gloria Patri?

A. The Apostles, according to Baronius in his 3d Tome.

Q. 1053. Why do we join unto the Gloria Patri, Sicut erat, &c. As it was in the beginning, is now, and ever shall be, world without end?

A. Because it was made by the Council of Nice against the Arians, who denied Christ to be coequal and consubstantial to his Father, or to have been before the blessed Virgin Mary.

Q. 1054. Why after this, for a great part of the year, and especially between Easter and Whitsuntide, do we say, Alleluia, Alleluia?

A. Because that is a time of joy, and Alleluia is a Hebrew word, signifying, "Praise ye the Lord with all joy, and exultation of heart."

Q. 1055. Why were it not better changed into English?

A. Because it is the language of the blessed in heaven, according to Apoc. Viii. 6. Therefore the church hath forbidden it to be translated into any other language.

Q. 1056. Why in Lent, and some other times, do we say, instead of Alleluiah, "Praise be to thee, O Lord, King of eternal Glory?

A. Because those are times of penance; therefore God must be praised rather with tears, than exaltation.

Q. 1057. Why then do we always say, for the invitatory Hail Mary, full of grace, the Lord is with thee?

A. To congratulate and renew the memory of our blessed Lady's joy, conceived at the conception of her Son Jesus; and to invite both men and angels to do the like.

Q. 1058. What signify the five verses following the invitatory, which begin, Come let us exult unto our Lord?

A. The five wounds of Christ, from which all our prayer hath its force and merit, and in honour of which all those versions are said.

Q. 1059. What mean the Hymns?

A. They are a poetical expression of prerogatives and praises of the Blessed Virgin.

Q. 1060. Why are so many Psalms used in the office?

A. Because they are directed by the Holy Ghost, and do contain in a most moving manner, all the affections of piety and devotion.

Q. 1061. Why are there but three Psalms in the most of the hours?

A. In honour of the most blessed Trinity, to whom chiefly the whole office is addressed.

Q. 1062. Why was the office divided into so many hours?

A. I have told you the chief reason already, and one other reason is, that so there might be no hour either by day or night, to which some hour of the office might not correspond.

Q. 1063. What do the matins correspond to?

A. To the first, second, and third watch of the night, consisting of three hours each; and therefore the matins consist of three psalms, and three lessons.

Q. 1064. What do the lauds correspond to?

A. To the fourth watch of the night.

Q. 1065. What do the prime, the third, sixth, and ninth hours correspond to?

A. To the third, sixth, and ninth hours of the day.

Q. 1066. What do the even-song and complin correspond to?

A. To the evening.

Q. 1067. What means the benedictions, or blessings given before the lesson?

A. They are short aspirations to beg divine assistance; and the first is in honour of the Father, and the second in honour of the Son, the third in honour of the Holy Ghost.

Q. 1068. What doth the lesson contain?

A. The mystical praises of our blessed Lady, taken out of the Prophets.

Q. 1069. Why do we end every lesson, saying, But thou, O Lord, have mercy upon us?

A. To beg the praises and virtues of the blessed Virgin, which we have there read, may be deeply settled in our hearts, and that God would pardon our former negligence, both in his and her service.

Q. 1070. Why is it answered, Thanks be to God?

A. To render thanks to God for his mercy, in bestowing such a patroness on us as the blessed Virgin Mary.

Q. 1071. What means the responsories?

A. They are so called, because they answer one another.

Q. 1072. What are the antiphons?

A. The versicles which are begun before the Psalms.

Q. 1073. Why do we stand up at the Magnificat, Benedictus, and Nunc dimittis?

A. To signify our reverence to the gospel whence they are taken.

Q. 1074. What is the collect?

A. It is a prayer, and is so called, because it collects and gathers together all the petitions and supplications of the whole office.

Q. 1075. Why is the collect always ended with these words, Through our Lord Jesus Christ, &c.?

A. To signify that he is our only mediator of redemption, and principally mediator of intercession; and that we cannot merit any thing by our prayers unless we make them in his name.

Q. 1076. Why make we a commemoration of the Saints?

A. To praise God in his Saints, according to the advice of the Psalmist, Psalm cl., and to recommend ourselves to their merits and prayers.

Q. 1077. Why end we every prayer with these words, And may the souls of the faithful, through the mercy of God, rest in peace?

A. That the poor souls in purgatory, may be partakers of all our prayers and supplications.

Q. 1078. Why is the whole office ended with some hymn or antiphon to our Lady?

A. That by her it may be presented to her Son, and by him to his eternal Father.

Q. 1079. Why are the nocturns in some offices so called?

A. Because those parts of the offices were wont to be said Nocturne tempore, in the night time.

Q. 1080. Why are the fifteen gradual psalms so called?

A. From a custom the Jews observed of singing them, as they ascended up fifteen steps or degrees (in Latin Gradus) towards Solomon's Temple, singing one psalm on every step.

Q. 1081. Why are the penitential psalms so called?

A. Because they contain many deep expressions of inward sorrow and penitence, or repentance of sins committed, and many cries or supplications to God for mercy and forgiveness.

# The Solemnities of CHRIST our Lord, (instituted for the most part by the Apostles) and the Sundays of the Year, expounded

Q. 1082. What meaneth the nativity of Christ, or Christmas?

A. It is a solemn feast or mass yearly celebrated by the whole Catholic Church from the Apostles' time to this day, in memory of the birth of Christ at Bethlehem; and therefore is called the feast of the Nativity, and Christmas from the mass of the birth of Christ.

Q. 1083. What meaneth the Circumcision or New-year's Day.

A. It is a feast in memory of the Circumcision of our Lord, which was made on the eighth day from his nativity according to the prescript of the old law, Gen. xviii. 12, when he was named Jesus according to What the angel had foretold, Luke i. 14, and began to shed his infant blood by the stony knife of Circumcision for the redemption of the world, presenting it to his Father, as a New-year's gift in our behalf. And it is called New year's day from the old Roman account, who began their computation of the year from the first of January.

Q. 1084. What meaneth the Epiphany, or twelfth day?

A. It is a solemnity in memory and honour of Christ's manifestation or apparition made to the Gentiles by a miraculous blazing star, by virtue whereof he drew and conducted three kings out of the East to adore him in the manager, where they presented him as on this day with gold, myrrh, and frankincense, in testimony of his regality, humanity, and divinity. The word Epiphany comes from the Greek, and signifies a manifestation, and is called Twelfth-day, because it is celebrated the twelfth day after his nativity exclusively.

Q. 1085. What meaneth purification or Candlemass-day?

A. It is a feast in memory and honour both of the presentation of our blessed Lord, and of the purification of the blessed Virgin, made in the Temple of Jerusalem the fortieth day after her happy child birth, according to the law of Moses, Levit. xii. 6. And is called the Purification, from the Latin word Purifico, to purify; not that our blessed Lady and contracted any thing by her child-birth, which needed purifying, (being the mother of purity itself) but because other mothers were by this ceremonial rite freed from the legal impurity of their child-births. And is also called Candlemass, or a Mass Candles; because before the mass of that day, the church blesses her candles for the whole year, and makes a procession with hallowed candles in the hands of the faithful, in memory of divine light, wherewith Christ illuminated the whole church at his presentation, where aged Simeon styled him, "A light to the Revelation of the Gentiles, and the glory of his people Israel." Luke ii. 32.

Q. 1086. What meaneth the resurrection of our Lord, or Easter-day?

A. It is a solemnity in memory and honour of our Saviour's resurrection, or rising from the dead on the third day, Matt. xxvii. 6. And is called Easter, from Oriens, which signifies the East or Rising, which is one of the titles of Christ, "And his name (saith the prophet) shall be called Oriens." Zach. vi. 12, because as the material sun daily ariseth from the East, the sun of justice, at this day, arose from the dead.

Q. 1087. What meaneth ascension-day?

A. If is from a feast in memory of Christ's ascension into heaven the fortieth day after his resurrection, in the sight of his Apostles and Disciples, Acts i. 9, 10, there to prepare a place for us, being preceded by whole legions of Angels, and waited on by millions of Saints, whom he had freed out of the prison of Limbo. Mich. ii. 13.

Q. 1088. What meaneth Pentecost or Whitsuntide?

A. It is a solemn feast in memory and honour of the coming of the Holy Ghost upon the heads of the Apostles, in tongues as it were of fire, Acts ii. 3. Pentecost in Greek signifieth the Fiftieth, it being the fiftieth day after the resurrection. If is also called Whitsunday from the Catechumens, who were clothed in white, and admitted on the eve of this feast to the sacrament of baptism. It was anciently called Wied Sunday, (i.e.) Holy Sunday, for wied or withed signifies Holy in the old Saxon language.

Q. 1089. What meaneth Trinity Sunday?

A. It is the octave of Whitsunday, and is so called in honour of the Blessed Trinity, to signify that the works of our redemption and sanctification then completed, are common to all the three persons.

Q. 1090. What meaneth Corpus Christi day?

A. It is a feast instituted by the church, in honour of the body and blood of Christ, really present in the most holy sacrament of the Eucharist; during the octave of which feast, it is exposed to be adored by the faithful in all the principle churches of the world, and great processions are made in honour of it; and therefore is called Corpus Christi day, or the day of the body of Christ.

Q. 1091. What meaneth the transfiguration of our Lord?

A. It is a feast in memory of our Saviour's transfiguring himself upon Mount Tabor, and showing a glimpse of his glory to his Apostles, St. Peter, St. James, and St. John. "And his face (saith the text) shown as the sun, and his garment became white as snow," &c. Matt. xvii. 2. And in them also unto us, for our encouragement to virtue, and perseverance in his holy faith and love. The entymology is obvious from transfiguro, to transfigure, or to change shape.

Q. 1092. What is Sunday, or the Lord's Day in general?

A. It is a day dedicated by the Apostles to the honour of the most holy Trinity, and in memory that Christ our Lord arose from the dead upon Sunday, sent down the holy Ghost on a Sunday, &c. and therefore is called the Lord's Day. It is also called Sunday from the old Roman denomination of Dies Solis, the day of the sun, to which it was sacred.

Q. 1093. What are the four Sundays of Advent?

A. They are the four Sundays preceding Christmas day, and were so called by the church, in memory and honour of our Saviour's coming both to redeem the world by his birth in the flesh, and to judge the quick and the dead; from the Latin word Adventus, which signifies Advent, or coming.

Q. 1094. What are the four Sundays of Septuagesima, Sexagesima, Quinquagesiam, and Quadragesima?

A. Those days are appointed by the church for acts of penance and mortification, and are a certain gradation or preparation for the passion and resurrection of Christ, being so called, because the first is the seventieth, the second the sixtieth, the third the fiftieth, the fourth the fortieth day, or thereabouts, preceding the octave of the resurrection according as their several names import.

Q. 1095. Why is the whole lent called Quadragesima?

A. Because it is a fast of forty days, in imitation of Christ's fasting in the desert forty days and forty nights, and is begun the fortieth day before Easter, which is therefore called Quadragesima, or the fortieth.

Q. 1096. What is Passion-Sunday? A. That is a feast so called from the passion of Christ then drawing nigh, and was

ordained to prepare us for a worthy celebrating of it.

Q. 1097. Why is Palm-Sunday so called?

A. It is a day in memory and honour of the triumphant entry of our Lord into Jerusalem, and is so called from the palm branches, which the Hebrew children strewed under his feet, crying Hosanna to the Son of David, Matt. xxi. 15. And hence it is that yearly, as on that day, the church blesseth Palms, and makes a solemn procession in honour of the same triumph, all the people bearing Palm branches in their hands.

Q. 1098. What is Dominica in albis, commonly called Low-Sunday?

A. It is the octave of Easter-day; and is so called from the Catechumens, or Neophytes, who were on that day solemnly divested in the church of their white garments.

# The Feasts of our Blessed Lady, and the Saints, Expounded

Q. 1099. What means the conception, nativity, presentation, annunciation, visitation, and assumption of our blessed Lady?

A. They are feasts instituted by the church in memory and honour of the mother of God, but chiefly to the honour of God himself; and so are all the other feasts of Saints.

Q. 1100. How explain you that answer?

A. The feast of the Conception is in memory of her miraculous conception, who was conceived by her parents, St. Joachim and St. Anne, in their old age, and sanctified from the first instant in the womb. The Nativity is in the memory of her happy and gloriousbirth, by whom the author of all life and salvation was born to the world. The Presentation, in memory of her being present in the Temple at three years old, where she vowed herself to God, both soul and body. The Annunciation is in memory of that most happy embassy brought to her by the angel Gabriel from God, in which she was declared to be the mother of God, Luke i. 31, 32. The Visitation is in memory of her visiting St. Elizabeth, after she had conceived the Son of God, at whose presence St. John the Baptist leaped in his mother's womb, Luke i. 41. And her Assumption is in memory of her being assumed or taken up into heaven, both soul and body, after her dissolution or dormition; which is a pious and well-founded tradition in the church.

Q. 1101. For What end are the several solemnities of Saints?

A. They are instituted by our holy mother the church, to honour God in his Saints, and to teach us to imitate their several kinds of martyrdoms and sufferings for the faith of Christ, as also their several ways of virtue and perfection: as the zeal, charity, and poverty of the Apostles and Evangelists; the fortitude of the martyrs the constancy of the confessors; the purity and humility of the virgins, &c.

Q. 1102. What meaneth the feast of St. Peter's installing and erecting his apostolical chair in the city of Antioch.

A. It is kept in memory of St. Peter's installing and erecting his apostolical chair in the city of Antioch.

Q. 1103. What is the feast of his chair at Rome?

A. It is a solemnity in honour of the translation of his chair from Antioch to Rome.

Q. 1104. Why are St. Peter and St. Paul joined in one solemnity?

A. Because they are principle and joint co-operators under Christ in the conversion of the world, St. Peter converting the Jews, and St. Paul, the Gentiles;

as also because both of them were martyred at he same place Rome, and on the same day, June 29.

Q. 1105. What means the feast of St. Peter and Vincula, or St. Peter's Chains?

A. It in in honour of those chains wherewith Herod bound St. Peter in Jerusalem, and from which he was freed by an angel of God, Acts xii. by only the touch whereof great miracles were afterwards effected; to say nothing of their miraculous joining together many years after into one chain, with those iron fetters, with which they had been imprisoned in Rome.

Q. 1106. What meaneth the feast of Michaelmas?

A. It is a solemnity or solemn mass in honour of St. Michael, prince of the heavenly host, and likewise of all the nine orders of holy angels; as well to commemorate that famous battle fought by him and them in heaven, against the dragon and his apostate angels, Apoc. xii. 7. in defence of God's honour; as also to commend the whole church of God to their patronage and prayers. And it is called the dedication of St. Michael, by reason of a church in Rome, dedicated on that day to St. Michael, by Pope Boniface. There is another feast called the apparition of St. Michael, and is in memory of his miraculous apparition on Mount Garganus, where by his own appointment, a temple was dedicated to him in Pope Gelasius' time.

Q. 1107. For What reason hath the holy church ordained a solemnity in memory of all the Saints?

A. That so at least we might obtain the prayers and patronage of them all, seeing the whole year is much too short to afford us a particular feast for every Saint.

Q. 1108. What meaneth All Souls Day?

A. It is a day instituted by the church, in memory of all the faithful departed, that by the prayers and suffrages of the living, they may be freed out of their purgatory pains, and come to everlasting rest.

Q. 1109. What means Shrove-tide?

A. It signifies a time of confession; for our ancestors were used to say, we will go to the shrift, instead of we will go to confession, and in the more primitive times all good Christians went to confession, the better to prepare themselves for a holy observation of Lent, and worthy receiving the blessed sacrament at Easter.

Q. 1110. What signifies Ash-Wednesday?

A. It is a day of public penance and humiliation in the whole church of God, and is so called from the ceremony of blessing ashes on that day, wherewith the priest signeth the people, with a cross on their foreheads, giving them this wholesome admonition, Memento homo, &c. Remember man that thou art dust, and to dust thou shalt return. So to prepare them for the holy fast of Lent, and passion of Christ.

Q. 1111. What means Maundy Thursday?

A. That is a feast in memory of our Lord's last supper, where he instituted the blessed Eucharist, or sacrament of his precious body and blood, and washed his disciples' feet; and it is called Maundy Thursday, as it were mandatum or mandat Thursday from the first word of the Antiphon, mandatum novum de vobis, &c. John xiii. 34. "I give unto you a new command, (or mandat) that you love one another, as I have loved you;" which is sing on that day in the churches, when the prelates begin the ceremony of washing their people's feet, in imitation of Christ's washing his disciple's feet, before he instituted the Blessed Sacrament.

Q. 1112. What meaneth Good-Friday?

A. It is a most sacred and memorable day of which the great good work of our redemption was consummated by Christ on his bloody cross.

Q. 1113. What means the three days of Tenebræ, before Easter?

A. It is a mournful solemnity, in which the church laments the death of Christ; and is called Tenebræ or darkness, to signify the darkness which overspread the face of the earth, at the time of his passion, for which end also the church extinguisheth all her lights, and after some silence, at the end of the whole office, maketh a great and sudden noise, to represent the rending the veil of the Temple. The darkness also signifies the dark time of the night wherein Christ was apprehended in the garden, and the noise made by the soldiers and catch-poles at their seizing on our Saviour's person.

Q. 1114. What meaneth Rogation week, being the fifth after Easter?

A. It is a week of public prayer and confession for the temperateness of the seasons of the year, and the fruitfulness of the earth, and it is called Rogation from the verb Roga, to ask by reason of the petitions made to God in that behalf.

Q. 1115. What means the Quatuor tempora, or four Ember weeks, or Ember Days?

A. Those are times also of public prayer, fasting, and processions partly instituted for the successful ordination of the priest and ministers of the church, and partly, both to beg and render thanks to God for the fruits and blessings of the earth. And are called Ember days, or days of Ashes, from the no less ancient than religious custom of using hair-cloth and ashes, in time of public prayer and penance; or from the old custom of eating nothing on those days till night, and then only a cake baked under the embers or ashes, which was called, Panis, subcineritius, or Ember bread.

Q. 1116. What mean the two Holy Rood Days?

A. Those are two ancient feasts: the one in memory of the miraculous invention, or finding out the holy cross by St. Helen, mother of Constantine the great, after it had been hid and buried by the Infidels one hundred and eighty years, who had erected a statue of Venus in the place of it. The other in memory of the exaltation, or setting up the holy cross by

172

Heraclius the emperor, who having regained it a second time from the Persians, after it had been lost fourteen years, carried it on his own shoulders to Mount Calvary, and there exalted it with great solemnity; and it is called Holy Rood, or Holy Cross, for the great sanctity which it received by touching and bearing the oblation of the most precious body of Christ; the word Rood in the old Saxon tongue, signifying Cross.

# Some Ceremonies of the Church Expounded

Q. 1117. What is holy water?

A. A water sanctified by the word of God and prayer. 1 Tim. iv. 5, in order to certain spiritual effects.

Q. 1118. What are those effects?

A. The chief are, 1. To make us mindful of our baptism, by which we entered into

Christ's mystical body, and therefore we are taught to sprinkle ourselves with it as often as we enter the material Temple (which is a type thereof to celebrate his praise.) 2. To fortify against the illusions of evil spirits, against whom it hath great force as witnessed Theodoret, Eccl. Hist. I. 5, c. 31. And hence arose the proverb, He loves it, (speaking of things we hate) as the Devil loves holy water.

Q. 1119. How ancient is the use of Holy water?

A. Ever since the apostles' time; Pope Alexander I. who was but the fourth Pope from St. Peter, makes mention of it in one of his epistles. Exod. xxxvii. 8., 2 Par. iv. 6.; 4 Kings ii. 21.; Ps. I. 9.; Heb. ix. 19.; x. 22; De Cons. Dist. iii. c. 20; B. Greg. Pastor, Pars ii. c. 5.

Q. 1120. Why is incense offered in the church?

A. To raise in the mind of the people an awe of the mysterious in the action to which it is applied, and to beget a pious esteem of it, as also to signify, that out prayers ought to ascend like a sweet perfume in the sight of God. "Tis mentioned by St. Dionysius, Eccles Hierarch. c. 3.

Q. 1121. Why is the cross carried before us in procession?

A. To show that our pilgrimage in this life is nothing but a following of Christ crucified.

Q. 1122. Why are our foreheads signed with holy ashes on Ash Wednesday?

A. To remind us of What we are made, and to admonish us to do penance for our sins, as the Ninevites did in fasting, sackcloth, and ashes, especially in the holy time of Lent.

Q. 1123. Who ordained the solemn fast of Lent?

A. The twelve Apostles, according to Heirom Epist. ad Marcel, in memory and imitation of our Saviour's fasting forty days.

Q. 1124. Why are the crosses and holy images covered in time of Lent?

A. To signify that our sins (for which we then do penance) interpose between God and us, and to express an ecclesiastical kind of mourning in reference to our Saviour's passion.

Q. 1125. Why is a veil drawn between the altar-piece and the people in Lent time?

A. To intimate, that, as our sins are as a veil which binder us from seeing the beatific vision, or face of God; and as the veil of the Temple was rent at the death of Christ, so is the veil of our sins by virtue of his cross and passion, if we apply it by worthy fruits of penance.

Q. 1126. What means the fifteen lights set on the triangular figure on Wednesday, Thursday, and Friday in holy-week?

A. The three upper lights signify Jesus, Mary, and Joseph; the twelve lower, the twelve Apostles. The triangular figure signifies, that all light of grace and glory is from the blessed Trinity; and fourteen of those lights are extinguished on by one after every Psalm, to show How all their light of spiritual comfort was extinguished for a time in those most Holy Saints, by the passion and burial of Christ. The fifteenth light is put under the altar to signify his being in the sepulchre, as also the darkness that overspread the whole earth at his death.

Q. 1127. What signifies the noise made after a long silence, at the end of the office of Tenebræ?

A. The silence signifies the horror of our Saviour's death; the noise, the cleaving of the rocks and rending the veil of the Temple which then happened.

Q. 1128. Why is the paschal candle hallowed and set up at Easter?

A. To signify the new light of the spiritual joy and comfort, which Christ brought us at His resurrection; and it is lighted from the beginning of the Gospel till after the communion, between Easter and Ascension, to signify the apparitions which Christ made to his disciples during that space.

Q. 1129. Why is the font hallowed?

A. Because the Apostles so ordered it, according to St. Dionysius, who lived in their time.

Q. 1130. Why is that ceremony performed at the feast of Easter and Whitsuntide?

A. To show that, as in baptism we are buried with Christ, so by virtue of his resurrection, and the coming of the Holy Ghost, we ought to rise again, and walk with him in newness of life.

Q. 1131. Why is the material church or temple hallowed?

A. Because it bears a figure of the spiritual, viz. the mystical body of Christ, which is holy and unspotted, Ephes. v. 27. as also to move us to some special reverence an devotion in that place, and all things should be holy in some measure, which appertain t the service of our most Holy God.

Q. 1132. Why is the altar consecrated?

A. Because if the altar in the old law was so holy that it sanctified the gift, Matt. Xxiii. 19. much more ought the altar of the new law to be holy, which is the place of the body an blood of Christ, according to Optatus, in his sixth book against Parmenian the Donatist "We have an altar (saith St. Paul) whereof they (the Jews) have no power to eat, wh serve the Tabernacle." Heb. xiii. 10.

THE END

Printed in Great Britain
by Amazon